THE ABUELOS

CUBAN ORAL HISTORY

COLECCIÓN CUBA Y SUS JUECES

EDICIONES UNIVERSAL, Miami, Florida, 2018

JOSÉ B. FERNÁNDEZ
UNIVERSITY OF CENTRAL FLORIDA

THE ABUELOS

CUBAN ORAL HISTORY

Copyright © 2018 by José B. Fernández

First Edition in English, 2018
(First Edition in Spanish, 1987 by Ediciones Universal)

EDICIONES UNIVERSAL
P.O. Box 450353 (Shenandoah Station)
Miami, FL 33245-0353. USA
(Since 1965)

e-mail: ediciones@ediciones.com
http://www.ediciones.com

Library of Congress Catalog Card No.: 2017952356
ISBN-10: 1-59388-289-0
ISBN-13: 978-1-59388-289-1

Text preparation: María Cristina Zarraluqui

Cover design: Luis García Fresquet

Photo on the cover: great-grandparents of the author, don José Josende and doña Josefa Dieste.
Also in the cover, Sagua la Grande's School of the Sacred Heart of Jesus (Jesuit) and on the inside back cover, Sagua la Grande's train station.

All rights reserved.
No part of this book may be used or reproduced
in any manner whatsoever without written permission
except in the case of brief quotations embodied in critical
articles or reviews. For information contact
Ediciones Universal.

To P.J., Michael, and Sophia.
May they be proud of their Cuban heritage.

ACKNOWLEDGEMENTS

First, and foremost, I would like to thank Provost Dale Whittaker and the Office of Academic Affairs at the University of Central Florida for granting me the Professional Development Leave which made the translation possible. I am also grateful to my friend Dr. Jorge Febles, a noted Cuban-American scholar from the University of North Florida for writing the Prologue for the translation. A kind note of gratitude goes to Ms. Carole González for reviewing the manuscript, my daughter Denyse Fernández Wilkins for typing the manuscript, and my wife Mimi for her support. I would also like to record with thanks the assistance of Dr. Enrique Casero, Frank Fernández, Eduardo Febles, Dr. Alberto Hernández Chiroldes, Eddie Fiol, Manuel García Ávila, Clarisa Miller, the Municipio de Sagua la Grande en el Exilio, Martha Pardo Sotolongo, Manuel Salvat, Margarita Sánchez Núñez and Alina VanTassel in providing photos of Los Abuelos.

In addition to thanking those whose invaluable contributions to the work who have already been acknowledged, I would like to thank Mr. Manuel Salvat, Publisher of Ediciones Universal for the publication *Los Abuelos: Cuban Oral History*. Finally, my deepest appreciation to all of the Abuelos.

TABLE OF CONTENTS

PROLOGUE 11

INTRODUCTION 19

THE ABUELOS 21

FIRST PART: MY LIFE IN CUBA 25
    Cuba 27
    Reminiscences of my Ancestors 31
    Blessings, Lullabies, and Childrens' Prayers 44
    Family Discipline 48
    My School 51
    Childhood Games 56
    Tricks, Pranks, and Punishments 60
    Youth Pastimes 64
    Courtships of Yesteryears 74
    Baptisms, Wakes, and Eulogies 79
    Christmas and Holy Week 83
    Feast Days, Holidays, and Carnivals 88
    My Hometown Memorable Folk Characters 94
    My First Job 99
    Meals, Sweets, and Beverages 103
    Remedies 108
    Stores 111
    Comets, Hurricanes, Fires, and Calamities 114
    Superstitions, Rites, and Ceremonies 121
    Cuban Legends 125
    Blacks, Chinese, Spanish, And Haitians 132
    The Cuban *Guajiro* 146
    Pimps and Human Trafficking 153
    Bandits 156

SECOND PART: CUBA AND ITS HISTORY 159
    The War of Independence.. 161
    Cuban Patriots.. 173
    The American Occupation of Cuba 182
    Estrada Palma's Arrival and Maximo Gómez's Funeral ... 185
    The 1906 "Little War" 187
    Estenoz's and Ivonet's "Little Race War" 190
    Liberals and Conservatives... 193
    The "Chambelona" Uprising 197
    The 1921 Economic Crisis... 200
    Machado's Dictatorship and the Hotel Nacional Episode... 202

THIRD PART: UNDER A FOREIGN SUN 211
    My Life In The United States 213
    Reflections 215

REFERENCES 219

PROLOGUE

Los abuelos Three Decades Later

When in 1988 I reviewed José B. Fernández's *Los abuelos: historia oral cubana* (Ediciones Universal, 1987) for *Cuban Heritage*, the cultural magazine edited by Miguel A. Bretos, I remember lamenting that since the book was entirely in Spanish, it would not be available to English-speaking historians in the United States and beyond. They would lack ready access, therefore, to the testimonies of those elderly exiles interviewed by the author in methodological fashion. Indeed, upon perusing the bibliographies and footnotes of such quintessential monographs centering on the evolution Cuban society as Louis A. Pérez Jr.'s *On Becoming Cuban: Identity, Nationality, and Culture* (1999), Richard Gott's *Cuba: A New History* (2004), Lars Schoultz's *That Infernal Cuban Republic* (2009), and Lillian Guerra's *Visions of Power in Cuba* (2012), to cite but four serious studies evincing exhaustive research, the reader fails to encounter any reference to *Los abuelos*. This seems ironic, particularly since such works are by and large self-conscious artifacts, consistent with the narrative quality of contemporary historiography. In other words, rather than replicating or contesting exclusively textual *truisms* of an academic nature, they rely as well upon a multiplicity of secondary cultural sources, often secured orally and emanating at times from individuals once or twice removed from the original informant. Thus, any modern English-speaking historian intent on delving into the early decades of the Cuban republic would profit from consulting an engaging compilation of memories like *Los abuelos*. Now, fortunately, thirty years removed from its date of publication, *Los abuelos* resurfaces in English not only to inscribe itself more vigorously within academia, but also to secure wider dissemination among the reading public due to its intrinsic general appeal.

In recasting the book, since as Gustavo Pérez Firmat implies any effort at interlingual translation encompasses a transformational endeavor and hence relative disloyalty to the mother tongue (*Tongue Ties* 2), Fernández has endeavored to remain faithful to the voices of those individuals to whom he posed questions long ago. Enrique Casero, Ricardo Cobián, Graciela DuBrocq, Ceferino García, Manuel García Iglesias, María Elba González, Hortensia López, Félix Medinilla, Carlos Montero, Josefina Pérez, Ana Aurora Recio, Felipe Roloff, Rodolfo Sotolongo, Celestino Suárez, Mario Vega, Víctor Vega Ceballos, Concepción Vigo and Lorenzo Zequeira —twelve men and six women born between 1888 and 1919— acquire just as convincing voices in English as they did in their recorded Spanish due to the author-translator's successful efforts to imbue them with appropriate conversational naturalness and spontaneity. All have died, a reality that fixes their statements forever in a precise time period and inheres in them an element of *pathos* already present in their initial testimonies. The diminishing hope regarding their forsaken homeland that they evinced in the 1980s now must be perceived as irredeemably lost, having vanished with them upon their demise. For instance, Josefina Pérez (over ninety one surmises at the time of the interview, since she was born in 1891) attests: "I miss Cuba a lot, and I would like to see it again. […] I would like to return to Cuba if it were to be free again, but I don't think that's going to happen. I think I'm going to die without ever returning to Cuba." The moving truth latent in her assertion makes her a character within a narrative construct, rather than the quite mortal elderly conversant she perceived herself to be when she spoke into Fernández's tape recorder in the 1980s. Therefore, the book now reads —albeit unlyrically— as a sort of Thomas Gray's "Elegy Written in a Country Churchyard," or Edgard Lee Master's *Spoon River Anthology*, or Elena Garro's play *Un hogar sólido*. In this version of *Los abuelos*, we visit with the dead from its inception, since Fernández makes it a point to underscore at the beginning the dates of birth and death of his subjects, asking the reader to undertake, therefore, a somewhat nostalgical excursion into the past of those long gone who in 2017 may be perceived as *bisabuelos* (great grandparents) or even *tatarabuelos* (great great grandparents) of potential readers, since those who first encountered this text like I did in 1988 wear at present that "hurricane survivor's face" ("Nochebuena," *The Last Exile* 3) distorted by too many *Nochebuenas* that once gazed upon us lovingly, to paraphrase once again Gustavo Pérez Firmat. We may currently be the *abuelos*, but that does not belie the book's perennial authenticity and documental worth.

As he underscores in the introduction, Fernández works on the basis of a tacit questionnaire made self-evident by section titles and subtitles, as well as by the responses provided. He wisely eradicates his authorial voice to allow his informants freely to voice ideas and stories at times divergent, at times complementary so as to create a panoramic view of the environment whence they evolved. Some have more knowledge than others about specific events; some experienced differently societal realities or historical developments. Particularly relevant in this regard are the opinions of women vis-à-vis men, as well as statements or stories grounded on financial or class-based status in prerevolutionary Cuba. For instance, interviewees like Víctor Vega Ceballos played an important role in the nation's affairs, while others like Ana Aurora Recio, daughter of Cuban War of Independence general Lope Recio, Felipe Roloff, grandson of General Carlos Roloff, and Rodolfo Sotolongo were descendants of recognizable historical figures. Yet, their discourse intermingles readily with those of the other informants to forge an inviting pastiche that intertwines high and low culture, significance and insignificance, history and tradition, facts and popular mythology. Divided in three main segments ("My Life in Cuba," "Cuba and Its History," and "Under a Foreign Sun"), *Los abuelos* creates a kaleidoscopic portrayal of the Cuba inhabited by these *grandparents* prior to their exodus, invariably depicted in heart-rending fashion. Yet, the speakers' recollections do not betray bitterness, but rather a conscious effort to instruct the listener (and by extension the readers) in order to chronicle, if succinctly, the life they lived in the island and in the United States.

Interviewees discuss notable events, local folklore, economic crises, traumatic personal circumstances, and so forth. Therefore, the narrative concocted on the basis of their recollections fluctuates between exuberance and chaos, detachment and passion, joy and tragedy, all circumscribed to a time period defined by the implied author's specific and often peculiar (I use the word with positive rather than pejorative intent) concerns that in historical terms encompasses the period between the War of Cuban Independence (1895-1898) and the collapse of the Gerardo Machado dictatorship (1933). Of course, the informants' remembrances of their own roles within Cuban society as children or as adults and the manner in which they recreate the environment —local or otherwise— where they grew up, resided, and afterwards forsook, distorts this chronological quasi-structure. Memories expand the time frame and confer vitality to the emerging narrative, given that they belong to displaced persons who submitted themselves to permanent exile in Miami.

By its very nature, the book's initial segment is by far the longest and most subjective. Speakers take up multiple inconsequential topics, such as games, home remedies, superstitions, rituals, courtship stratagems, traditions, holiday celebrations and such at the same time that they ponder the fortunes of famous bandits and peasants, or tenuous racial relations. Comprised of many picturesque anecdotes, this section impresses because of its sociocultural significance. For instance, while reading many an ephemeral personal tale one discovers that in the early 1900s most private tutors in Camagüey were educated blacks, or that the exclusive Atenas Club in Havana only accepted whites if they fulfilled demanding educational criteria. Felipe Roloff recounts in picturesque detail and comic parsimony commonplace rural obsequies, while Hortensia López clarifies somewhat unconsciously the naiveté integral to early twentieth century romantic practices. Other informants refer to Holy Week processions, Judas burnings, physical punishments applied to misbehaving children, tales pertaining to famous bandits like Manuel García, Matagás and

"Los Gallos," and even proffer lessons on how the *zapateo* should be danced.

"Cuba and Its History" deviates only slightly from the charming national or regional idiosyncrasies depicted in the first part of *Los abuelos*. In this segment, speakers refer to serious historical events surrounding the birth and growing pains of the Cuban nation, but they do so spontaneously, which confers to their voices authority not devoid of prejudiced self-centeredness. In other words, the author-translator allows interviewees to address events that interest him and by extension the reader without intervening, permitting their statements to resonate coherently or incoherently as normal utterances produced by real human beings. Witness for example Felipe Roloff's version of the 1906 upheaval that brought about the second United States intervention into Cuban affairs:

> I know the true story of "La guerrita de 1906" (The 1906 "Little War") because my grandfather was the Treasurer of the Cuban Republic under Don Tomás Estrada Palma. Everything started when Don Tomás decided to go up for reelection and his opponents didn't like that. I don't think it was his ego which prompted him to make that decision. On the contrary, I think he did it out of his sense of duty and in good faith.

Afterwards he adds: "I know all of this because my father told me that his grandfather had told him the whole story." Although Rodolfo Sotolongo and Josefina Pérez respond with their own memories of the so-called *guerrita*, their opinions pale when juxtaposed to the "true story" told emphatically by Roloff. As such, these recollections framed against each other by the author turned listener-organizer enhances the narrative appeal of the text.

Logically the shortest, the third and final section of *Los abuelos* consists of brief praise on the part of informants for the country that welcomed them as refugees, supplemented with reflections by a select few, those whose judgments enticed the implied listener-organizer: Josefina Pérez, Rodolfo Sotolongo, Carlos Montero, Hortensia López, Ceferino García, Ricardo Cobián, and Víctor Vega Ceballos. In essence, upon contemplating a life well lived, all underscore their gratitude with faint self-praise. Having lost the capacity to effect change, the *abuelos* nevertheless do not pine for days gone by, conscious as they are of the ineluctable movement of the clock hands. Once again, these reflections add poignancy to the book because they truly emerge from the grave.

To conclude, *Los abuelos* is a grand book, a praiseworthy paean to things past. Postmodern thinking notwithstanding, lawyer Gavin Stevens assertion in Faulkner's *Requiem for a Nun* that "The past is never dead. It's not even past" (73)resonates powerfully when confronting an oral history project such as the one undertaken by José B. Fernández, especially when after thirty years his informants' voices sound as vigorous as they did previously in the informants' Spanish. Fiction writer Roberto G. Fernández once told an interviewer concerning the publication of his first novel in English, *Raining Backwards*: "When I was writing the book, I wanted to leave some sort of record of this generation that's dying, that's disintegrating" (p. 12). He referred, of course, to the impending demise of those older Cubans like his parents that comprised the initial exodus from the island in the 1960s and 1970s. In his English translation of *Los abuelos*, José B. Fernández does him one better: he resurrects a prior generation, the parents of those now disappeared or disappearing parents, to make them assert their humanity and experiences once more. As such, he has created not only an indispensable book for scholars of modern Cuban history, but also an everlasting tribute to those eighteen individuals that acquiesced to address his tape recorder so very long ago.

Dr. Jorge Febles
University of North Florida

WORKS CITED

Faulkner, William. *Requiem for a Nun*. Reprint. New York: Penguin Random House, 2012.

Fernández, José B. *Los abuelos: historia oral cubana*. Miami: Universal, 1987.

Gott, Richard. Cuba: A New History. New Haven and London: Yale UP, 2004.

Guerra, Lillian. *Visions of Power in Cuba: Revolution, Redemption, and Resistance, 1959-1971*. Chapel Hill: The U of North Carolina P, 2012.

Photos, Lisa. "Author Tells Immigrants' Story." *Florida Flambeau*. April 20, 1988, p. 9 and 12.

Pérez Firmat, Gustavo. *The Last Exile*. Georgetown, Kentucky: Finishing Line Press, 2016.

____. *Tongue Ties: Logo-Eroticism in Anglo-Hispanic Literature*. New York: Palgrave Macmillan, 2003.

Pérez Jr., Louis A. *On Becoming Cuban: Identity, Nationality, and Culture*. Chapel Hill: The U of North Carolina P, 1999.

Schoultz, Lars. *That Infernal Little Cuban Republic: The United States and the Cuban Revolution*. Chapel Hill: The U of North Carolina P, 2009.

INTRODUCTION

Abuelos (grandparents or senior citizens) are living books. They possess a wealth of information that is not found in library books. They pass along that information in an entertaining manner, with vigor, joy and enthusiasm.

In 1987, I published *Los abuelos: historia oral cubana*, a book whose purpose was that of serving as a source of information for those interested in Cuban history and culture. It consisted of a series of interviews with a heterogenous group of eighteen elderly Cuban exiles, representing all of the island's regions. Although the individuals came from diverse social origins, they all knew how to tell a grandfatherly story.

The book was divided into three parts: "My Life in Cuba," consisting of the Abuelos' reminiscences ranging from family traditions to courtship customs; "Cuba and Its History", a part focusing solely on the period between the War of Independence (1895-1898) and 1933; and "Under a Foreign Sun", a reflection of their lives in the United States, and their lives in general. It was topically organized to make it more interestingly to the reader. Therefore, some of the "abuelos" were more explicit than others regarding the described topic.

Essentially, the book belonged to the Abuelos. All I did was to transcribe what they told me and how they told me. Some editing, however, was necessary and changes were made in order to improve the quality of the narratives.

In an effort to provide an English translation for those interested in Cuban history and culture, as well as for generations of Cuban-Americans whose first language is English, I am providing this translation so that they can be proud of their Cuban heritage and ensure that these voices from the past are not forgotten.

The art of translation from one language to another is not an easy task and *The Abuelos* has proven to be no exception. Since *The Abuelos* is an attempt to preserve history as testimony, the Spanish imperfect tense, so commonly used in Spanish, predominates throughout the translation. Additionally, English contractions are used reflecting the linguistic authenticity of the stories. Definitions and explanations are provided the first time a Spanish word or term appears unless there are customary Spanish words used in English. Capitalization of Spanish words into English follow current accepted practices; however, capitalization is often used as a means of signaling and emphasizing the importance of a tile or an event, instead of following a set of grammatical conventions. Poems, riddles, prayers, sayings and lullabies in Spanish are not literally translated. An effort has been made to preserve their rhyme without losing their ingenuity and authenticity.

Footnotes containing biographical and geographical information of people and places mentioned in the narratives are provided, as well as historical notes clarifying assertions made in the narratives whenever necessary.

The names of the Abuelos, their birthdates, birthplaces and other information can be found in "The Abuelos" section of the translation. All of the "Abuelos" have departed, but their testimonies have left an indelible mark in Cuban history.

This translation is neither a masterpiece nor an example of stylistic perfection; it is rather an expression of the Abuelos's deep love for Cuba. To all of them, my debt of gratitude.

THE ABUELOS

ENRIQUE CASERO
    Born: June 26, 1903
    Place: Santiago de Cuba, Oriente Province
    Died: March 5, 1991
    Place: Miami, Florida

RICARDO COBIÁN
    Born: March 30, 1895
    Place: Pinar del Río, Pinar del Río Province
    Died: March 3, 1993
    Place: Miami, Florida

GRACIELA DUBROCQ
    Born: February 4, 1902
    Place: Matanzas, Matanzas Province
    Died: March 22, 1990
    Place: Miami, Florida

CEFERINO GARCÍA
    Born: March 19, 1898
    Place: Terlova, Asturias Province, Spain
    Died: November 15, 1993
    Place: Miami, Florida

MANUEL GARCÍA IGLESIAS
    Born: February 17, 1911
    Place: Sagua la Grande, Las Villas Province
    Died: July 5, 1986
    Place: Miami, Florida

MARIA ELBA GONZÁLEZ
    Born: August 3, 1904
    Place: Remedios, Las Villas Province

Died: February 12, 1992
Place: Miami, Florida

HORTENSIA LÓPEZ
Born: May 29, 1988
Place: El Caney, Oriente Province
Died: May 30, 1985
Place: Miami, Florida

FÉLIX MEDINILLA
Born: June 20, 1896
Place: Trinidad, Las Villas Province
Died: December 1985
Place: Miami, Florida

CARLOS MONTERO
Born: October 4, 1891
Place: Havana
Died: March 4, 1987
Place: Miami, Florida

JOSEFINA PÉREZ
Born: June 15, 1891
Place: Cienfuegos, Las Villas Province
Died: December 31, 1995
Place: Miami, Florida

ANA AURORA RECIO
Born: May 30, 1903
Place: Camagüey, Camagüey Province
Died: September 5, 1993
Place: Miami, Florida

FELIPE ROLOFF
Born: May 26, 1912
Place: Morón, Camagüey Province
Died: July 30, 2011
Place: Jefferson, North Carolina

The Abuelos

RODOLFO SOTOLONGO
    Born: November 3, 1901
    Place: Colón, Matanzas Province
    Died: December 10, 1985
    Place: Miami, Florida

CELESTINO SUÁREZ
    Born: June 11, 1901
    Place: Cienfuegos, Las Villas Province
    Died: June 2, 1989
    Place: Lansing, Michigan

MARIO VEGA
    Born: June 1, 1919
    Place: Havana
    Died: March 12, 1988
    Place: Miami, Florida

VÍCTOR VEGA CEBALLOS
    Born: January 22, 1901
    Place: Camagüey, Camagüey Province
    Died: June 26, 1996
    Place: Miami, Florida

CONCEPCIÓN VIGO
    Born: October 21, 1911
    Place: Mayarí, Oriente Province
    Died: January 5, 2003
    Place: Miami, Florida

LORENZO ZEQUEIRA
    Born: September 5, 1904
    Place: Havana
    Died: June 30, 1988
    Place: Miami, Florida

FIRST PART

MY LIFE IN CUBA

CUBA

CEFERINO GARCÍA: I'm Spanish, and all my records show that I'm Spanish. But all of my feelings are in Cuba. Every night, despite the fact that I left Cuba a few years ago, I dream about Cuba. I dream about the friends that I left there, those who are alive and those who are dead. Cuba is something that is very dear to me, and saying something about Cuba to me, is like saying something about my true family. I love Cuba.

CONCEPCIÓN VIGO: Cuba is my constant thought, my ideal, my life. It's everything for me. I do not like to talk about it, but I'm always thinking about Cuba. There is something peculiar about my longing for Cuba and that's the fact that since I left Cuba, I can't sing the Cuban national anthem. Everyone sings it, except me. I can't sing the national anthem because I start crying.

RODOLFO SOTOLONGO: Cuba, for me, is everything because I'm a true Cuban in the sense that I've never criticized it. I always believe that Cuba was the best country in the world. I long for its landscape, its music, and its women's beauty. All are reasons why I love my country.

JOSEFINA PÉREZ: I miss Cuba a lot, and I would like to see it again. Over there, everything was fine. We were very happy and living over there was fine. However, Cuba now is hell. I would like to return to Cuba if it were to be free again, but I don't think that's going to happen. I think I'm going to die without ever returning to Cuba.

VÍCTOR VEGA CEBALLOS: Every time I think about Cuba, I feel that it is talking to me. What does it tell me? Well, it tells me many things and it asks me many things. It proposes to me many things and I begin to think. When the word Cuba is mentioned, I feel I'm watching a silent movie. I watch the Cuban veterans and patriots in front of me and I watch everything that happened in Cuba. I watch the hardships Cubans had to endure in establishing a great nation and I also watch all of the bad things that befell on us due to our political bickering and inability to get along. It's always better to compromise than to have a revolution. Generally, revolutions destroy more than they create and they give evildoers the opportunities to commit injustices.

MARÍA ELBA GONZÁLEZ: For those of us who were fortunate to be born in Cuba, we can only remember one word: Cuba. Columbus rightly said that Cuba was the most beautiful land that he had ever seen. There is not a single day that I don't remember Cuba, my homeland. That's what keeps me here in exile from becoming an American citizen. It's like the lines from one of the exiled poet's poems: "Thank you, Yankee, but I'll never be an American. If I die and were to be born again, I'll always be Cuban."

MARIO VEGA: When I hear the word Cuba, I see myself and my homeland, the country that Martí[1] dreamt establishing, the country Carlos Manuel de Céspedes[2] wanted, the country General Antonio Maceo[3] fought for. I miss Cuba very much. I miss its green fields

---

[1] José Martí y Pérez (1853-1895). The most important figure in Cuban history and one of the greatest authors in Latin American literature. Born in Havana, on January 28, 1853, he died at the battle of Dos Ríos, Oriente Province, on May 19, 1895

[2] Carlos Manuel de Céspedes (1818-1874). Known as the "Father of the Country," he started the ill-fated Ten Years' War of Cuban Independence (1868-1878). Born in Bayamo, Oriente Province, on April 18, 1819, he died at the Battle of San Lorenzo, Oriente Province, on February 27, 1874.

[3] Antonio Maceo y Grajales (1845-1896). General of the Ten Years' War, and second-in-command in the Cuban War of Independence (1895-1898). Born in Santiago de Cuba, Oriente Province, on June 4, 1845, he died at a skirmish in Punta Brava, Havana Province, on December 7, 1896.

in the Cuban morning mist. I miss its starry night and its sea. Cuba is its landscape and its beauty. In summary, it's everything that surrounds it. Cuba is something marvelous, especially for one who lived there, for one who wept for it, for one who longed and suffered for it. The homeland is unforgettable, simply unforgettable.

LORENZO ZEQUEIRA: I'm Cuban from head to toe. Cuba, for me, is everything. Incidentally, yesterday, I was talking with someone near my home and he told me: "Look at the beautiful blue sky." I replied: "Yes, but that sky is neither as blue nor as starry as the one in my homeland. I don't know why, but, here, in this country, you never see a star at night."

FELIPE ROLOFF: For me, Cuba is the greatest country in the world. My biggest wish is to die in Cuba because it's my homeland and there is nothing like Cuba. Cuba was a small country, but it was a great country. We Cubans used to say that one could live underneath a rock and still have a great life. Cuba is in my blood because I came from a *Mambí*[4] family.

MANUEL GARCÍA IGLESIAS: For my well-being, I've tried to erase Cuba from my mind. But, I really can't because all my dreams take place in Cuba. For me, Cuba means my roots.

HORTENSIA LÓPEZ: Columbus said that Cuba was the most beautiful land ever seen by human eyes, and he was right. I love Cuba very much, but I will never see it again.

---

[4] Word used by the Cuban patriots during the Ten Years' War of Independence and the War of Cuban Independence as a symbol of pride. Some opine that it's derived from the name of Eutimio Mambí who fought against the Spanish in Santo Domingo prior to leaving for Cuba. Others maintain that it's an African word meaning "son of a monkey." It appears that it was brought over from Santo Domingo and that the Spanish used it to derogate Cuban patriots.

CARLOS MONTERO: It hurts me very much that we have lost Cuba. Despite its many shortcomings, it was the best country in the world. I've been to many countries, but I've never lived in a place as great as Cuba.

Carlos Montero, c. 1950s
(Courtesy of Margarita Sánchez Núñez)

REMINISCENCES OF MY ANCESTORS

ANA AURORA RECIO: I was born on May 30, 1903, in the city of Camagüey and my parents were Lope Recio y Loynaz and Ángela Malvina Silva Zayas. I come from a *Mambí* family. My paternal grandfather was José Agustín Recio y Loynaz. He was Ignacio Agramonté's[5] cousin. My father was a Major General in the Cuban War of Independence and Governor of Camagüey Province, once Cuba was proclaimed a republic in 1902.

My father was an exceptional individual. He was a brave man who had both character and integrity. He was the type of person who never lost his cool. He was a happy man who loved parties. He was simply a good-natured guy, beloved by many people. I remember that often, black soldiers under his command during the War of Independence, would come to visit him and one of them would say: "General, I just came by to see you, just to give you a big hug." Once he would leave, my father would tell us: "You see that black man, I gave him a hug. I get a greater pleasure by shaking his hands, than by shaking the hands of white Cubans who are nothing but trouble makers." I also remember that when one of our servants accidentally would break something, he would never get mad. He would simply get up from his rocking chair and tell her: "Don't worry, shopkeepers need to make a living, don't worry about it."

My father was a loving man. He never got angry. He was good-natured and had to be good-natured in order to command 5000 men during the War of Independence. He was such a brave

---

[5] Ignacio Agramonte y Loynaz (1841-1872). Major General in the Cuban Ten Years' War and one of its most important heroes. Born on December 23, 1841, in Camagüey, he died at the Battle of Jimaguayú, Camagüey Province, on May 11, 1872.

man. We have a letter from Máximo Gómez[6], telling my father that he was invaluable to the independence cause, thanking him for his fight for Cuban freedom. At the end of the letter he wrote: "Lope Recio is unique, because he's a very brave man."

CEFERINO GARCÍA: I'm a full-blooded Asturian[7], but a Cuban at heart. I was born in Terlova, an Asturian village, on March 19, 1898, but I immigrated to Cuba on December 20, 1915. I lived in Cuba until October 10, 1966. My father was Ramón García López and my mother was Rosa González Campa. My father was born in the same house where I was born. My mother, on the other hand, was born in San Cristóbal de Entreviñas, near Avilés.

JOSEFINA PÉREZ: I'm a bit old because I was born in 1891, a few years before the War of Independence started. My mother was named Elvira Gómez González, and she was from Manzanillo, Oriente Province. My father was Jesús Pérez Cristián; he was also from Oriente Province. I think he was from Contramaestre, but I'm not sure.

    I hardly knew my mother because she died when I was four years old. She died in Cienfuegos, Las Villas Province, where I was born. As for my father, I came to know him when I was older because when the War of Independence started, he went to fight. I remember that he was short and a bit fat. Everyone called him *"El Mambí,"* because he had been a sergeant with the *Mambises*.

    My aunt, Juana González Fonseca, was the one who raised me. She was my grandmother's sister. She used to tell me that my maternal grandparents had come from Maracaibo, Venezuela, to Cuba, because of war over there. She would tell me that before

---

[6] Máximo Gómez (1836-1905). General in the Ten Years' War and Commander-in-Chief of the Cuban Liberation Army during the War of Independence. Born in Baní, Dominican Republic, on November 18, 1836 he died in Havana, on June 17, 1905.

[7] From Asturias, a region in northwestern Spain.

they left for Cuba they hid their money and jewelry under their parish church's floor in Maracaibo. They were hoping to return, but they never did. They first went to Manzanillo and later to Cienfuegos.

RODOLFO SOTOLONGO: I was baptized as Rodolfo Teófilo Sotolongo Vila at the parish church in Colón, Matanzas Province. I was born in Colón on November 3, 1901. I was the youngest of Gerardo Sotolongo's and María Eugenia Vila's four children. I'm a descendant of one of Colón's founders. According to records, a group of landowners from Vega Bermeja, Matanzas Province, founded the town of Colón. One of those founders was my maternal great-grandfather. All of my maternal relatives were landowners. My mother, for example, was born at the "Favorito" sugar mill, owned by my grandfather. As to my paternal grandparents, they were Antonio Sotolongo and Mariana Franchi Alfaro y Vargamachuca. They were from Havana but I never got to know them.

GRACIELA DUBROCQ: I'm Pío Dubrocq's and Engracia Romero's daughter. I was born in the city of Matanzas, on February 4, 1902. My paternal grandfather was a Frenchman who immigrated to Matanzas and founded Versalles District in Matanzas. He named it Versalles because it reminded him of Versailles, near Paris. Since he was an engineer, he built the Concordia Bridge, which links Versalles with Matanzas. Before that bridge, the only way to cross the river was by boat. Since he did so much for Matanzas, the city donated to him part of the La Cumbre District along with some land along the coast where the docks bearing his name are located.

My grandfather never returned to France. In one of the trips we took, we went through Bayonne where my grandfather was born. One of the avenues over there is named Dubrocq Avenue. The Dubrocqs are one of the oldest families in that city. I spoke with some of the people from that city and they told me that one of the Dubrocqs left for Cuba but never returned. I would have liked to meet my French cousins, but they were not there when we went to Bayonne. As to my parents, my father owned several properties and my mother was a piano teacher. I believe that's where I get my passion for piano.

FÉLIX MEDINILLA: My parents were black. My father, just like me, was born in Trinidad. He was named Francisco Medinilla and my mother's name was Apolonia Pichardo. I don't know what my father did for a living, but my mother was a laundress. She washed with her own hands. I don't remember much about my family, because I don't have any brothers or sisters. My parents died when I was very young. The only family I have is the one I've raised. I have seven children, five of them living in Cuba, and two living here in the United States. I was born on July 20, 1896.

HORTENSIA LÓPEZ: I soon will cease to exist because I was born on May 29, 1888. I was born on a farm named "La Dolorita," near El Caney, Oriente Province. I don't know how long it took in our horse cart to El Caney, but at that time trips took very long. The roads were rocky and trips could only be made by horse carts.

    My father was Francisco López Fernández. He was Spanish and had a bakery and general store. My father was a very energetic and a tough man because one had to be tough to support a family of eight, right in the middle of the War of Independence. As for my mother, she was named Filomena de La Rosa y Torres. She was a very honest woman and very industrious because she was always doing something with her hands.

    I never knew my paternal grandparents. They were Asturians who remained in Asturias. I knew my maternal grandparents who were from the Canary Islands. My grandfather was Gabriel de la Rosa and my grandmother was Ignacia Díaz. My poor grandmother died in the Canary Islands. Although she lived in Havana, she went there to claim an inheritance. Unfortunately, she contracted pneumonia on the trip and just as she was getting off the ship, she died. The inheritance was nothing –just a few *tostones*[8] of little value.

After my grandmother died, my grandfather went to live with us when I was about 14 years old. I remember him well. He was always doing something. He was a cabinetmaker. Although he was old, he would always be fixing tables' wooden pegs and filling seat covers with straw. He loved to read and his favorite book was *El libro del año 2,000*[9]. He was fascinated with the things that were in that book. Today, we have many things that appeared in that book.

VÍCTOR VEGA CEBALLOS: I was born at six in the morning on January 22, 1901, in Camagüey. My parents were Ángel Vega Beltrán and Luisa Ceballos Muñoz. During the War of Independence, my father was in charge of communications between Camagüey and the rest of the island. After the war he was a court clerk.

My father was influential with the workers because he had been a baker during his youth. He, along with my uncle Liborio Vega, Agusto Betancourt Pichardo and Nicolás Guillén[10], founded the Camagüey Workers' Union. It was a small organization because there weren't that many industries in Camagüey. However, the bakers, for example, would listen to him. Whenever he said: "Let's go on strike!", they went on strike. Whenever he said: "Stop the strike!", they stopped.

As to my paternal grandparents they were Don Pedro Vega, a Frenchman, and Doña Mercedes Beltrán, a Canary Islander. This Frenchman came to Camagüey with a basket on his head sell-

---

[8] A *tostón* was a silver coin used during Spanish colonial times, equivalent to 50 cents. The plural is *tostones*.

[9] The book's real title was in *In The Year 2889*. Recent research indicates that its real author was Michael Verne, Jules Verne's son.

[10] Nicolás Guillén Urra (1864-1917). Cuban politician and father of the famous Afro-Cuban poet Nicolás Guillén (1902-1989). He was also a senator from Camagüey Province.

ing plastered saint figures. Then he established a prosperous business and sold it to Don Anselmo Simoni, Ignacio Agramonte's wife's grandfather.

Regarding my maternal grandparents, they were Don Julián Ceballos and Doña Ana Josefa Muñoz de Álvarez Cisneros. She, by the way, was related to the Marqués de Santa Lucía[11]. My grandfather was Cuban just like my grandmother, but my grandfather was Franciso de Ceballos Vargas's[12] son, who had been Spanish Vice Governor of Cienfuegos. This man had been in Cuba for 15 years and was named Interim Captain–General of Cuba. According to many, he was a very honest man and also a monarchist. He was not very popular because he was very strict and didn't like catering to people.

I only got to know my paternal grandmother Doña Mercedes and what I remember most about her was her height. She was a very tall Canary Islander and very serious. She became a widow when she was young. She lost her husband and two sons in the 1851 Conspiracy[13]. I remember that she didn't use any form of transportation; she went on foot wherever she went. No one could tell her: "Doña Mercedes, Víctor is suffering from asthma," because she would take her shawl and walk to our home which was about two kilometers away. Once she arrived she would begin shouting orders like: "Start heating water and get a washbasin to give him a bath now!" "Hey, bring me some warm olive oil to put on his chest!" The minute I was getting well, she would put on her shawl and go to some other relative's home to help them out.

---

[11] Nobility title of renowned Cuban patriot Salvador Cisneros Betancourt. Born in Camagüey, on October 10, 1868, Cisneros Betancourt was President of the Republic in Arms during the War of Cuban Independence. He was later a senator from Camagüey Province. He died in Havana, on February 28, 1914.

[12] Francisco de Ceballos Vargas (1814-1883). He was Captain-General of Cuba from 1872 until 1873.

[13] Name given to the ill-fated conspiracy against Spanish colonial authorities in Cuba, led by Joaquín de Agüero. Captured in a battle with Spanish troops, Agüero, along with his followers, were executed by Spanish authorities on August 12, 1851.

"Ah! How I remember her!" She was a very stoic woman. Right now I'm seeing her in front of me, sipping chicken broth and eating a piece of fatback. She never had high cholesterol and none of these illnesses that we see today. She lived until she was ninety-five years old. If she hadn't fallen down, Doña Mercedes would be here today.

RICARDO COBIÁN: In my family, we were three brothers and three sisters. My father was a merchant and he had the largest store in Pinar del Río, the city where I was born on March 30, 1895. My father was named Ricardo Cobián Beltrán Benítez. They were from La Coruña, Spain. My mother, on the other hand, was from Pinar Del Río, but she lived for a few years in Spain, while her brother studied to be an army officer. My mother's name was Narcisa Vera Silva and her brother, José Vera Silva, even became a Spanish army general and served in Cuba.

CARLOS MONTERO: I'm part Spanish and part Italian. My father was named Juan Antonio Montero, he was Vicente Montero's son, a Spanish sailor. My father, just like my mother, Herminia Ruga, was born in Havana. My mother was Carlos Ruga's daughter, Italian Consul in Havana.

    I never knew my paternal grandparents, but I got to know the one who was consul. He fought alongside Garibaldi[14] in Italy. I know this because I kept some of his memorabilia which, unfortunately, I left behind in Cuba. My grandfather, every time he would be near our home, would have a pocketful of candy and we would run after him throughout the Vedado District streets. They were not really streets, but rather a bunch of dusty roads.

    We were four brothers and there are only two of us left, me, born in Havana, on October 4, 1891 and a younger brother, a dentist who lives in Cuba. Apparently, he likes the Castro regime,

---

[14] Giusseppe Garibaldi (1807-1882). He is known as the "Hero of Italian Independence."

so, I wrote him a letter the other day, letting him have it. We were always a close family. A long time ago, families were very close, very close.

MANUEL GARCÍA IGLESIAS: I'm from Sagua la Grande, Las Villas Province, and I was born on February 17, 1911. My father's name was Manuel García Montero, and he was a butcher. My mother's name was Celia Iglesias Torres, and she was a homemaker. My paternal grandfather was Manuel García and he was from the Canary Islands. My paternal grandmother was Concepción Montero, she was Cuban. My maternal grandfather was named Antonio Iglesias. He was a Galician[15] from El Ferrol, and he had a general store in Sagua, called "El amigo de los niños." ("The Kids' Friend"). My maternal grandmother was Luz Torres and was from Remedios, Las Villas Province.

  I spent some time with my maternal grandmother. She was a very interesting person. Once my grandfather died, she lost the business. She was a widow with four children and no financial resources. She only had the small home where she lived. Since she had a small sewing machine, she became a seamstress. Her income as a seamstress enabled her to help her children get through. I'll always be thankful to her and all the knowledge I got from her.

CONCEPCIÓN VIGO: My parents were 100 percent Spanish who emigrated to Cuba at the beginning of the 20th century. I was born in Mayarí, Oriente Province, on October 21, 1911, but when I was two or three years old we moved to Guantánamo, so I'm a *Guantanamera.*

  My father was born in Villaba in Galicia's Lugo Province, and my mother was born in Gavilanes, near Ávila, Spain. The interesting thing about my parents was their love for Cuba. They always spoke nicely about Cuba and were happy there because they got married and started a family. Cuba, rather than Spain, was

---

[15] From Galicia, a region in the northwest corner of Spain.

their country. My father became a Cuban citizen in 1926. My mother felt so Cuban that when we went into exile via Spain, I wanted to take her to her hometown, but she didn't want to go and kept saying to me: "No, I don't want to go, all I want is to return to Cuba."

MARIO VEGA: I never had the opportunity to know my grandparents. I heard they were from the Canary Islands. My father was named Ramón Vega González, and my mother's name was Rosario Díaz Cabral. My father was from Güines, Havana Province, and my mother was from Matanzas.

We were five brothers and five sisters and I was born on June 1, 1919. The thing I most remember about my father is that he was a very quiet man, and just by looking at one of us, he could tell it all. He could had been wealthy because prior to the War of Independence he had a charcoal business and a drycleaners one, but he left everything. He wanted to help the Cuban patriots and was totally committed to Cuban independence. As a matter of fact, he was wounded in the leg and never fully recovered. The wound caused his death years later.

My mother, on the other hand was not as quiet as my father. She was quite a seamstress who made beautiful *guayaberas*[16] and laced dresses. She saved everything because we were a poor family. She raised us in a very Cuban and Christian way, and was responsible for guiding us through life.

LORENZO ZEQUEIRA: I was born in Havana, on September 5, 1904. I was the son of Lino Zequeira Lafontaine and Manuela Pastrana Paroli. My paternal grandfather was Erundino Zequeira and my maternal grandparents were José Pastrana and Donata Paroli. I have Spanish, black and French blood. The surname Lafontaine is

---

[16] According to sources, the *guayabera* is a traditional Cuban dress shirt with patch pockets and vertical rows of seven pleats running the length of the entire shirt.

French and one of my ancestors was a Frenchman who came to Oriente and owned a few coffee plantations.

I was the oldest of three brothers. Perhaps, because I was the oldest, my father was very fond of me. I was very fond of him too. Even after I got married, I would visit him every day. I would quickly leave Havana City Hall, where I worked, and go to Santos Súarez District just to have lunch with my father. He was always waiting for me. I was very fortunate that he died right on my chest. I believe that all parents love their children equally, but there is one child who is the first among equals.

ENRIQUE CASERO: My full name is Juan Enrique Casero Vega, and I was born on June 26, 1903. My parents were both from Santiago de Cuba. They were Francisco Casero Seriol and Aurelia Vega Zunzunegui. My maternal grandfather was General Matías Vega[17], who was the one who accepted the Spanish Morro Castle's surrender in Santiago de Cuba.

Matías Vega was a brave man, but my uncle José Vega Zunzunegui, known as "Veguita" was even braver. He rose against the Spanish and was captured. Thanks to the Jamaican Ignacio Hernández's efforts, he was paroled. Well, when Ignacio was with him on the train, that bastard jumped out and began shouting to the Spanish soldiers on the train: "Sons-of-bitches, come out and fight me! My father is operating around here. Let's see if you want to fight him. You are a bunch of chickens!" It's true that his father's troops were at El Cristo's area in Oriente Province. By the end of the war, he became a *Mambí*, officer. Later on, in one of the many Cuban uprisings he got killed. He went after his cousins' assassins and they ambushed him around La Maya, Oriente Province, and killed him in cold blood. My uncle, "Veguita," was really brave, really brave.

---

[17] General Matías Vega was not the one who accepted the Spanish Morro Castle surrender at Santiago de Cuba. However, he was the Cuban Liberation Army's representative who raised the Cuban flag at the castle when the American occupation of Cuba (1898-1902) ended on May 20, 1902.

The Abuelos

CELESTINO SUÁREZ: I have a very long name – José Antonio Celestino Suárez Santander. I was born in Cienfuegos, on June 11, 1901. My parents were Manuel Suárez Pérez and Carmen Santander Romero. My father was a butcher and my mother was a homemaker. Three of my grandparents were from Trinidad. They were Pablo Santander, Carmen Pérez and Susana Romero. However, my paternal grandfather, just like my father, was from San Martín de Luna, a little village in Asturias Province.

I never knew my grandparents but my parents told me about them. My father was a hard-working Spanish man, and although he had been a *Voluntario*[18] during the War of Independence, he never had any problems with the Cubans. He had a butcher shop and would always get up at three in the morning because the sugar-transporting barges' captains would come to buy beef before departing from port at five in the morning. Later, at around eleven or so, he would come home, shower and go to the slaughterhouse to buy dressed cattle for the shop. He would close his shop at eight in the evening. However, the day wasn't done, because he would go to the restaurants to collect money they owed from purchasing beef on credit. It's funny, he would give them credit in the morning and collect the money in the evening. After making his rounds, he wouldn't arrive at home until nine or ten in the evening. He would always bring us –we were five boys and five girls– delicious pastries called Santo Domingo pastries.

Regarding my mother, she was nearly five feet tall and heavyset. She had a temper but she was good to us. I remember that when I was nine, she used to wake me up by saying: "Get up, and go to your father's butcher shop to watch over the beef packets so that no one steals them." As I was going out, she would say: "Make sure you walk right on the middle of the street, so that I can see you." I did what she told me to do and I'm grateful to her.

---

[18]*El Cuerpo de Voluntarios* (Volunteer Corps) was a paramilitary vigilante group mostly made up of Spanish residents in Cuba. Its main mission was to help Spanish authorities on the island during the 19th century.

MARÍA ELBA GONZÁLEZ: Remedios, in Las Villas Province, is one of the oldest towns in Cuba, and right there was where I was born on August 3, 1904. My father was named Rafael González Rojas and my mother was named Rosa Bravo de Guzmán Abreu. My paternal grandparents were from Remedios and their names were Rafael González and Arcadia de Rojas y Pantaleón. My maternal grandparents were Rosa González Abreu y Ortegosa and Eusebio Bravo de Guzmán y Jiménez. My grandfather was Spanish, but my grandmother was an Abreu, a family who owned several sugar mills in Las Villas.

I can honestly state that I came from a *Mambí* family. My grandaunt, Marta Abreu[19], my grandmother's sister, gave away all of her fortune for Cuban independence and all the Abreus participated in the war. Marta Abreu's husband, Luis Estévez, was Cuba's first vice president. I loved him very much.

The townfolks loved my grandmother Rosa. I remember that in my home, there was a huge bronze door. It would open in the morning and the whole town would come to say hello to her. I loved my grandmother above everyone else. She was my everything. Every day, I remember her. The last thing I did before I left Cuba was to visit my grandmother's grave.

FELIPE ROLOFF: I was born in 1912 at a farm near Morón, Camagüey Province. As one can notice, my last name Roloff is not Cuban, but my grandfather, despite not being born in Cuba was much more Cuban than many Cubans, because he fought in the War of Independence. He was Major General Carlos Roloff Mialovski.

My father, Gerardo Roloff, also fought in the War of Independence and when the war ended, he was on Generalissimo

---

[19]Marta Abreu Arencibia (1846- 1909). High society Cuban lady who made enormous contributions in financing military expeditions to Cuba during the War of Cuban Independence. She also distinguished herself for her philanthropic activities. She was born in Santa Clara, Las Villas Province, on November 13, 1846 and died in Paris, on January 2, 1909.

Máximo Gómez's staff. After the Cuban Liberation Army's mustering, he went to Morón and married my mother Tomasa Castillo, a Morón native. My father was born in Remedios and was a serious man. Regarding my grandparents, I only knew my maternal grandfather who was a great horserider.

As to the general, I have many anecdotes that my father told me. As everyone knows, he was Polish, and although he spoke seven languages, he spoke Spanish with a strong accent. He loved *plátanos* (plantains), but the poor man couldn't pronounce the word correctly and he called them *blátanos*.

He was born in Poland in 1842, but the Russians, who were a bunch of sons-of-bitches were occupying Poland at the time. So, he left for Germany, where he studied at a Naval Academy. My grandfather left Germany and came to the United States. In this country, he fought for the North in the American Civil War. He rose to the rank of captain in an Ohio regiment.

After the war, he came to Cuba and fought in The Ten Years' War with the rank of major general. In the War of Independence, he was the general that brought more armed expeditions to Cuba. As a matter of fact, he, along with Rius Rivera[20], and Máximo Gómez, were the only foreigners who were granted the right to become Cuban president, but none accepted it[21]. He died almost in poverty in Guanabacoa, near Havana, in 1907, and yet he was Treasurer of the Cuban Republic. What an irony! He also wrote the *Índice del Ejército Libertador*, the official index of the Cuban Liberation Army.

---

[20] Juan Rius Rivera (1848-1926). Colonel in the Ten Years' War and major general in the Cuban War of Independence. After the war, he became Governor of Havana Province during the American occupation. He was born in Mayagüez, Puerto Rico, on August 26, 1848 and died in Honduras, on September 20, 1926.

[21] The 1901 Cuban Constitution recognized the contributions of four foreigners to Cuban independence by granting them the right to become president of Cuba. Among these foreigners were the Dominican Máximo Gómez, the Pole Carlos Roloff, the Puerto Rican Juan Rius Rivera and the Chinese José Bo.

BLESSINGS, LULLABIES, AND CHILDRENS' PRAYERS

VÍCTOR VEGA CEBALLOS: Every evening, right after supper, the children would go to the elders and ask one of them for his or her blessing. The one to be asked for a blessing was Juanita, my great-great grandmother's cousin. She would always be seated on her rocking chair. Even though she was half-senile, we respected her as if she were a goddess. She would make the sign of the cross and would say: "May God turn you into a saint." Afterwards, we would kiss her hand and go to sleep.

RODOLFO SOTOLONGO: Every evening, before going to sleep, we would ask our grandmother for her blessing. Afterwards, we would kneel by our beds and say a prayer to the Guardian Angel. It went like this:

> *Guardian Angel*
> *Sweet protector of mine*
> *Guard me during the night*
> *And tomorrow all the time.*

MARIO VEGA: When we went to sleep, my mother would sing us lullabies. She sang many of them, but my favorite was "Arrorró mi niño." ("Rock-A-Bye, Baby"). Every time she sang that lullaby, I went to sleep immediately.

GRACIELA DUBROCQ: My grandmother used to spend time with us and before we went to sleep, she would sing us a song. It wasn't a lullaby, it was a short song. I can't remember it very well but I think it went like this:

> *Grandma's hair is all grey*
> *And she teaches us how to pray*

*While mother sews
And father works
Grandma tells us stories
And we have no worries.*

**Graciela Dubrocq and Rodolfo Sotolongo, 1976
(Courtesy of Martha Pardo Sotolongo)**

CONCEPCIÓN VIGO: Before I went to sleep, they would tell me tales. I think they were Andersen's tales. When we were kids, my grandmother taught us a prayer. It was a simple one, but a beautiful one. It went like this:

To sleep, I'm all set
Four little angels guard my bed
And the Apostle Paul
Guards my soul.

CELESTINO SUÁREZ: All of us had to pray before we went to sleep. One of the prayers went like this:

My sweet child Jesus
I am a child like you
And I love you
From evil keep me apart
And I will give you all my heart.

MARIA ELBA GONZÁLEZ: In Remedios there was a character called "Masca Piedra" ("Rock Chewer"). He was the town's gravedigger. He usually would go around the streets, just about when children were ready to go to sleep, and would yell: "I eat little kids." Every time we heard that, we were terrified. I covered my head with a sheet and someone had to come and calm me down and say a prayer that went like this:

Four little angels will guard you through the night
And you'll have no fright
Have no fear
Go to sleep, Elbita dear.

MANUEL GARCÍA IGLESIAS: When we didn't want to go to sleep, they will try to scare us with "El Coco" ("The Bogeyman"). Of course, it was an imaginary figure, but we imagined him like sort of a monster. They would tell us: "The Coco is going to take you away, if you don't go to sleep right away."

CELESTINO SUÁREZ: My mother was very religious and whenever it was thundering she would tell us that it was God's wrath and say: "Lord, placate your wrath, sweet Jesus have mercy on us."

FELIPE ROLOFF: We had our share of bad storms at our farm. They were full of lightning, thunder, and lightning strikes. Whenever there was one of those storms, my mother would burn a piece a palm leaf that had been blessed on Palm Sunday, and would pray to Santa Bárbara. The prayer went like this:

Blessed be Santa Bárbara
Who are in heaven
Protect us with all your might
And deliver us from fright.

FAMILY DISCIPLINE

MANUEL GARCÍA IGLESIAS: One would not address the elders by using the tú familiar form; instead we had to use the usted polite form. In front of the elders we didn't use "choice" words and couldn't argue with them. All that sense of discipline was lost when Castro's revolution came to power. The current Cuban regime did away with all of the formalities we were used to when we were growing up.

CARLOS MONTERO: At home, we had tremendous respect for the elders. We weren't allowed to participate in their conversation. Even if they were wrong, we couldn't say anything. Today, everything is different. If you try to admonish a young one today, you are liable to be insulted. It's really sad. It's a real misfortune for this country.

VÍCTOR VEGA CEBALLOS: When the elders were having a conversation and a kid would approach them, one of the relatives would look at him or her, straight in the eyes and that meant "get out of the way." And, woe to the one who wouldn't get out of the way! Because, afterwards, came the spanking. If the kid was a male, they would pull his pants down and if it was a female they went, lifted her skirt up, and then, with a three-inch-thick belt, they would give him or her a well-deserved spanking.

MARIO VEGA: We always said grace during breakfast, lunch and dinner. My father would always tell us: "Children, whatever is served, I don't want to see anything left on that plate." We would never leave anything on the plate.

RODOLFO SOTOLONGO: Respect was something fundamental for all of us. No one sat at the table until my maternal grandmother sat. We had to wait for her to sit at the head of the table because that was her official seat. It was a way of honoring her because she was the oldest in the family. She, then, would say grace and we had to observe absolute silence. We had tremendous respect for my grandmother. There were things I didn't like to eat, but I had to eat them out of respect for her. For example, we would start the meals with soup because that was customary in Cuba. I didn't like soup, so many times I would ask the servant not to serve me soup. My grandmother would turn to the servant and say: "Instead of serving him two spoonfuls serve him three." She would then turn to me and say: "Young man, you must learn to have soup!"

FELIPE ROLOFF: At home, every time we ate, it was done in complete silence. We all had to wear a shirt, even if there was a two-year-old kid. My father always used a long sleeve undershirt, but when it was time to eat he would wear his guayabera. He was the first one to sit and afterwards he would sit in complete silence because he always said that God was present at the dinner table. There was so much silence, so much order.

CELESTINO SUÁREZ: My mother gave us a well-rounded education. I remember that once, when I was a bit older, I was seated at the table and said to the servant: "Vicenta, bring me coffee!" My mother turned to me and said: "Go and drink your coffee in the kitchen!" She then looked me straight in the eyes and said: "You forgot to say: Vicenta, would you please, bring me coffee." So, I had to drink my coffee in the kitchen because you didn't mess around with my mother.

HORTENSIA LÓPEZ: In Cuba, we had tremendous respect for the elders. Sure, some families were stricter than others, but in my home, even after I was married, there was absolute respect for the elders, especially for my father.

I am going to tell the story of what happened to me after I was married, so that people can see what I'm trying to say about discipline and respect: My husband and I loved to go to the theater.

One evening, before leaving for the theater, I came all dressed up to my parents' home. It was a striped cross over dress, but somehow, I forgot to pin it, so that the dress's low neck wouldn't show. My husband didn't tell me anything because he never paid attention to the way I dressed. However, my father, who would notice anything, said to my mother whose name was Filomena: "Filo, do you have a pin?" My mother replied: "Why do you want a pin now?" When he got the pin, he approached me and pinned my low-neck line so that nothing would show. I said to him: "C'mon, father, Enrique never pays attention to these things." He replied: "But, I do."

My husband used to say when we were courting and after we were married: "Anyone who comes to see Don Pancho better show absolute respect because no one messes around with him." The lack of respect that exists today didn't exist during my times. Of course, the years have gone by and many things have changed.

MY SCHOOL

RODOLFO SOTOLONGO: I first attended a small school ran by a school teacher's wife. I can't exactly recall her name, but everyone called her "Monina." Her maiden name was Hernández and her husband's name was Carlos Atalay. As a matter of fact, he later became my teacher in my last year of secondary school. The school was located on Nueva Street, right on the corner of Vilches Street in Colón. I still remember my classmates who used to walk to school with me. They were a black man's children and their last name was Fernández Torisa. The oldest one became a doctor and later was appointed Deputy Secretary of Health in one of Cuba's governing bodies.

I will always be thankful to that lady for teaching me how to read and write. She really had a lot of patience to put up with us. At times, she would punish us, but it was a rather symbolic type of punishment. Apparently, she had a renal ailment; she was also a seamstress. At that time, sewing machines were pedal operated, so our punishment was to go under the machine and push the pedal with our hands. By punishing us, she didn't have to push the pedal with her foot, which caused her pain. There was always a "punished" kid pushing the pedal. No matter what, I'll always remember her as a great teacher.

HORTENSIA LÓPEZ: My mother wanted me to learn about everything, and I'm grateful to both God and her. In Santiago de Cuba, there was a school located on San Basilo Street, between Reloj Street and Calvario Street. Its name was "Las Hijas de María." Every afternoon, right after lunch, I used to get dressed and go to class to learn embroidering. There were only three or four in that class. Many things that I know how to do today, I learned over there.

FELIPE ROLOFF: The school I attended was a public school which was about two kilometers from our farm. The school had been there since Spanish colonial times. The school principal's name was Rafael Acosta. He was a great teacher, and a great Cuban, who taught us about José Martí. During the Great Depression, he didn't get a paycheck because Cuba was undergoing a serious economic crisis. Yet that man never missed a day of work. Teaching was his sacred duty and he taught different generations of students. May he rest in peace.

GRACIELA DUBROCQ: I went to school at Irene de Toland for five years. The little English I knew, I learned it there. I didn't like English, but an American teacher would grab me by the chin and tell me "Speak English!" I would tell her: "Oh, yes! Oh, yes!" It was the best school in Matanzas. The education I received was magnificent. It was an American school with very qualified teachers. Afterwards, I went to Teachers' School which had just been established. They would only admit the top fifty students. I was admitted thanks to the education I received at Irene de Toland.

I still remember the songs and hymns I learned at that school because I was the one who played the piano. Before we began a class in the morning we had to sing a hymn. The school was a Protestant-run school. I remember one him that went like this:

> C'mon young people
> C'mon without delay
> Christ is unfolding his flag
> Throughout the nation
> He would lead us into battle
> C'mon without delay.

MARIO VEGA: At an early age, I went to public school. It was located on Monte Street, Cuatro Caminos. The teacher was named Rosaínz and he was very strict. He reminded me of José Martí because he was very just and fair. He was the epitome of respect. I went there from kindergarten to third grade. Some time later, I got a scholarship to San Alejandro School. I was an intern. Since I missed my parents so much, I escaped more than 16 times. Amado, the schoolmaster, used to tell me: "We are going to readmit you, because you are a brilliant student." However, I wouldn't pay attention and continued escaping.

I would run away from school and ask a taxi to take me to 29 Estévez Street, which was my home address. The taxi would take me, and there I was, sitting in the back and my parents would have to pay for it. By the way, they decided not to send me as an intern anymore, just as a day student. However, that didn't work out.

Afterwards, I went to Candler College, an American run school in Havana. I went there until the middle of the sixth grade, but when President Machado[22] fell from power, my father could no longer afford the tuition and I had to quit school. Whatever I know is what I've learned on my own. I'm a self-taught man.

CONCEPCIÓN VIGO: I remember that at elementary school we were taught *El manual de urbanidad*[23]. The teacher would ask us questions and we would have to answer according to the manual. We also had to behave according to what was prescribed in the manual. Now, in secondary school, the manual was no longer used, but all elementary schools, whether public or private, had to use it.

CARLOS MONTERO: I started at Belén Jesuit school. I was a very good student; I remember when President Don Tomás Estrada

---

[22]Gerardo Machado y Morales (1879-1931). Cuban president from 1925 until 1933. His dictatorship was one of the most repressive in Cuban history. He was overthrown on August 12, 1933. Born in Manajabo, Las Villas Province, on September 29, 1871, he died in Miami, on March 29, 1939.

[23]*El manual de urbanidad* was a manual providing rules for proper conduct for all occasions. It was written by Prof. Francisco Carreño (1818-1847). Carreño, a highly-educated individual, taught at the University of Havana.

Palma[24] visited the school and decorated me with a medal. I don't know why, but it must've been because Father Quevedo recommended me. Don Tomás always liked to visit schools because he was a former teacher.

I remember my classmates. There was Juan, a dark-skinned guy who was something else. I remember that we both got punished for getting into a fight. The teacher put us behind a tall cabinet where sports equipment was kept. Juan, was on one side, facing the wall, and I was on the other side also facing the wall. We, again, got into a fight and almost knocked down the cabinet.

I didn't last long at Belén because I got expelled for pushing Father Alonso down the choir staircase. It just happened that I was in the choir, but one day, while coming down the stairs, Father Alonso claimed that I had tried tripping him and he hit me on the head. I turned back and pushed him down the stairs. So, I got kicked out. From there, I went to the Escolapios School in Guanabacoa, but I lasted for a very little time there. Finally, I went to the Gran Antilla School and was there until I finished. The problem with me was that I was a very unruly kid.

JOSEFINA PÉREZ: I went to a private school. Matilde Salvadó was its owner and it was a good school. It was a school for boys and girls. It was on Zaldo Street. Matilde was the principal and there was a teacher named Rosa Rabasa who was a great teacher. In that school, we studied math and geography. In that class we had to memorize all the capitals in the world. If you didn't know the lesson, they would sit you in front of the class with a "Dunce" cap. For the ones misbehaving they made them kneel down with dried corn kernels under their knees.

VÍCTOR VEGA CEBALLOS: In Camagüey, it was usual for children to have private tutors. For example, for math, almost all of

---

[24] Tomás Estrada Palma (1835-1908). Cuba's first president (1902-1906). He was born in Bayamo, Oriente Province, on June 9, 1835, and died in Santiago de Cuba, on November 14, 1908.

the private tutors were blacks. I remember Don Tomás Vélez Vásquez, a huge black man, who was very modest and humble. He taught at his home and charged very little. At times, he would do it for free.

I guess Don Tomás seemed to embrace Unamuno's[25] saying of "even if I'm hungry, I'm in charge." For example, if he noticed that I wasn't coming to class and he would see me on the street, he would say: "Hey, why aren't you coming to class?" I would answer: "Well, Don Tomás, you know, things are tight at home; we have no money to pay you." He would reply: "I've never ever sent your family a bill nor have demanded a promissory note for my tutoring. Who has told your family that I'm so selfish an individual that I can't give what I have? The only thing I have is what I've learned, and give it freely. Look, come in right now and don't give any more excuses. Whenever I see your father, I'll talk with him and we will straighten things out. He has judged me wrongly."Don Tomás taught math, grammar, literature, history, geography, physics, chemistry, English and French. He was a formidable math teacher. He taught from Monday through Friday and only charged three *pesos*[26] a month.

For French, we had another black tutor, Prisciliano Garay. He was a black aristocrat who dressed in a white linen suit with a violet on his lapel. He only hung around with rich people.Another tutor was José Armando Plá, a mulatto. We used to call him "Pure Mathematics" because that's the way he advertised his tutoring business in the newspaper. Later on, he stopped tutoring and became a journalist and a lawyer. He was a great journalist who wrote brilliantly. He was very well respected. As a matter of fact, I have a picture where I'm giving him a hug.

---

[25] Miguel de Unamuno y Jugo (1864-1936). One of the greatest Spanish authors and philosophers of the 20th century and Rector of the University of Salamanca, Spain's first university. Born in Bilbao, on September 29, 1864, he died in Salamanca, on December 31, 1936.

[26] Cuban monetary unit, equivalent to the US dollar prior to 1959.

CHILDHOOD GAMES

CARLOS MONTERO: When I was in elementary school I used to play a lot of baseball. At that time, we used to play with a leather-covered rag ball. We used that type of ball until we could get a hold of a rubber ball. Getting a rubber ball for one was like becoming a general. We used to play baseball almost every day. We played in vacant lots because in the Vedado District, from 13th Street all the way up to 23rd Street, there was nothing but vacant lots. In fact, 12th St. didn't even exist.

We also played marbles and my friend Pedro Tejero and I used to play with the spinning top, going from one block to the other. Now, whenever we saw kids that weren't from my neighborhood we got into fights. They either had to fight me or my friend Pepe Cárdenas and sometimes both of us. Pepe Cárdenas, by the way, became Rector of the University of Havana. We simply didn't like those who were not from our neighborhood.

RICARDO COBIÁN: When I was a kid, I used to play with marbles and bottle caps. We also played politics. I was ten or eleven years old and we had an election at a house which my father owned. We elected Julio Escobar as president and José Nieto as Speaker of the House.

RODOLFO SOTOLONGO: We used to play army at our farm. We divided ourselves among the kids living in the farm. Some were the Spanish soldiers and the others were the *Mambises*. We would make wooden machetes and wooden horses which we rode on. Each side would charge the other and I remember there was a lot of hard-hitting with those wooden machetes.

I also remember that one of the first things I learned as a kid was to ride a horse. They bought me a pony and I would go hunting on horseback and sometimes on foot. I loved to go hunting. I had a single shot 22 caliber rifle and with that rifle I would go hunting around the fields. I used to hunt starlings, pigeons, crows and ravens.

ANA AURORA RECIO: I remember when I was a child, boys played with marbles and girls had jump ropes. The game I enjoyed the most was "La Marisola que está en su vergel" (Marisola is in her flower garden). We would hold hands and make a circle and one of us would be in the middle of the circle. We then sang "La Marisola," an old nursery rhyme and when we finished, we would break the circle, start running, and she would try to catch one of us.

MANUEL GARCÍA IGLESIAS: When I was a kid, I played with marbles right on the streets. They weren't really streets. They were rather dirt roads where there was no traffic. We would make a circle in the dirt, place the marbles there and with a bigger marble which was the shooting marble, you tried to knock as many of your opponents' marbles off the circle.

I also loved kite flying. The kid who lived across the street from me and I used to build our own kites. We made them out of thin wooden rods and thin paper. The big ones we made we called them *coroneles* (colonels). Once we built a kite, we would go down to the riverside and fly them. It was a lot of fun.

Another game we played was *quimbumbia*. It was a game played with a sawed-off broomstick. There was the larger piece which was sort of like a bat and smaller piece sharpened at both ends called the *quimbumbia.* It was placed horizontally in a circle right in the dirt. With the larger piece, one tried to hit the *quimbumbia.* as far as possible. If one missed, one was out of the game.

We enjoyed ourselves a lot without hardly having to spend anything. Things have really changed now. Today for example, buying Christmas gifts for a child is very expensive. One can easily spend $300 or $400 buying gifts.

MARÍA ELBA GONZÁLEZ: When I was a child, we played lots of games. There was one called *"El Periquín Pisao,"* which was a real fun game. It was similar to hide and seek. Everyone would hide and run to a selected place and the last one to arrive would be out of the game. So, we would call him *"Periquín Pisao,"* meaning you are out.

There was another game called *"¿Cuántos panes hay en el horno?"* (How many pieces of bread are in the oven?). We would make a circle and say a riddle that went like this:

> How many pieces of bread are in the oven?
> Twenty-five and one all burnt out
> Who burnt it?
> The mangy puppy
> Grab him, grab him!
> He's a glutton
> Throw him to the bottom.

We would then scramble out, and the side with the most kids on it was the winner.

LORENZO ZEQUEIRA: A very popular game was three bottle caps. The caps were flipped into the air and the one whose three caps landed upside down was the winner. We also played *quimbumbia* and baseball because we used to live on Industria Street which was not far from the *malecón* (seawall) and we played around there.

GRACIELA DUBROCQ: I always loved to rollerskate. Over at Martí Boulevard we used to roller-skate. We also played games. We played hide and seek. The girls played together and we never played with the boys.

MARIO VEGA: My parents were poor, so I made my own toys. Since I was an apprentice at Modesto Gómez's, carpentry shop in Havana, I could make my own toys. Actually, what I did there was to sweep the wood shavings. They allowed me to make scooters, trucks, blimps, and anything I wanted. One day, I made a wooden seaplane and they complimented me a lot.

**Mario Vega, 1979
(Courtesy of Alina Van Tassel)**

TRICKS, PRANKS, AND PUNISHMENTS

RICARDO COBIÁN: Some of the bad things we did were to jump neighbors' walls. I was one of the best jumpers and no one could catch me. Another bad thing we did was to go swimming in the river without letting anyone know about it. One time, Juanillo Montalvo and I went swimming in the river. However, his father, "Coquito" Montalvo, an army lieutenant, found us there, and things went bad for us. I ran home, and locked myself in my bedroom and didn't come out until things calmed down. Luckily, I wasn't punished. My father never punished me, because he didn't pay much attention to my behavior. My mother was the one who was in charge of discipline at home.

GRACIELA DUBROCQ: There was a guy who owned a produce store right on the corner where I lived. Five of us girls would tell our parents that we were going to visit his wife who lived upstairs. Really, what we would do was to go to the store and eat the finger bananas that were hanging from the store's ceiling. We would do this when he wasn't looking. That man loved me and he would always tell me: "You are the nicest and prettiest girl in all of Versalles." I would say to myself: "If you only knew all the bananas I ate while you weren't looking."

MARIO VEGA: I remember when I was a boy we would pull a number of pranks on Chinese fritter vendors. We would go around their stands with ice cubes and right when the lard was at its hottest temperature, we would throw the ice cubes right on the spot and run as fast as we could. The Chinese vendor would come running after us yelling and cursing.

    Another thing we did was to go around knocking on doors. In Cuba, some homes had huge door knockers, so, what we did was to knock as hard as we could and run away as fast as we could. The police knew who we were and what we were doing. There was one officer nicknamed "Lead Leg" because he couldn't run at all. However, he would grab his club and throw it right at our legs. If the club hit you, it hurt like hell. We had a lot of fun with our pranks.

ENRIQUE CASERO: I misbehaved at times, so my father bought a four-inch-thick-belt from Marcelino, the harness maker. However, he used it very few times because I would start running to a custard apple tree bordering my home's roof and I would jump from the tree to the roof and break a few tiles. One time I was caught and they put a gown on me and wearing that stuff I couldn't go out on the street.

RODOLFO SOTOLONGO: When one disobeyed, they would sit you on a chair and put you in timeout. They would put a red flannel gown on you, so that you couldn't go out on the street. I remember we never had a spanking because we had a lot of respect for our parents.

CARLOS MONTERO: They never punished me, but I was admonished many times because of all the tricks and pranks I used to do. I used to read stories about cowboys and Indians. After reading those stories I would try to imitate those characters. My friend, Julio Cárdenas, and I would go on horseback galloping at full speed, looking down at the grass, just like the Indians in the stories. It's a miracle we didn't kill ourselves. I could do that because I was strong and had muscles. The other day I looked at my muscles and all I have is bones because I'm 92 years old.

VÍCTOR VEGA CEBALLOS: Our family was a numerous one because my cousins lived with us. One of the tricks we used to do was faking an ailment so that we didn't have to go to school. However, my mother was very strict and at six in the morning she used to conduct an inspection tour to check who didn't want to go to school. If she noticed that someone wasn't up, she would ask:

"Why are you still in bed? Why haven't you gotten up?" He or she would reply: "Well, my stomach hurts a bit." She would ask: "So, you have a stomach ache!" She would then holler to the servant: "Francisca, please, bring me a spoonful of castor oil because we have to cure this poor child." The kid would reply: "No, no, I'm okay now." She would look straight at the child and say: "So, you are okay now, well, here take this spoonful of castor oil so you won't tell any more lies. You rascal, how do you dare to fake an illness so that you don't have to go to school?" You'll bet that kid wouldn't try to pull that trick again.

CARLOS MONTERO: A long time ago, men were not allowed to go to the theater without wearing long pants. There was a law that minors had to wear shorts. We were always trying to figure out how to get a hold of a pair of long pants so that we could go to the Alhambra[27]. People said that it was a risqué type of theater and that's why we wanted to go. So, we would ask our father's Galician servant to lend us his pairs of long pants. That's the way we would go there once in a while. The Alhambra was nothing compared to what I've seen later. In that theater, the actors danced and would tell a couple of double meaning jokes. That was all - it wasn't a trashy place.

MARIO VEGA: My father had a three-inch-thick-belt hanging under the Sacred Heart's portrait. I used to tremble every time I looked at that belt and hear my father saying: "If you misbehave, I'm going to hit your butt with it."

One time, I remember him hitting me with it because I did something terribly wrong. I lived on 29 Estévez Street and the Pilar Social Club was near there. People went dancing there. That place was so big that a thousand people could fit there. I was not even a teenager, but I always wanted to go there. One day, I fig-

---

[27] The Alhambra Theater opened its door in Havana on September 10, 1890 and closed in 1934. It was famous for its satire skits about Cuban politicians and double meaning jokes.

ured out how to get in. Since I was strong and tall, I looked much older than my age. So I took a piece of cork, burnt it a bit and ran it over my face. After a while, I had a moustache and a beard. I then put on my oldest brother's pair of pants which somehow fit me and went out.

I went near the place and watched the porter. At one point, when he wasn't looking I got in. I wasn't thinking about how mad my parents would be, because all I wanted to do was to dance with women who were older than me. My parents were very worried because they hadn't seen me. They went all over the neighborhood looking for me and couldn't find me. They were desperate. Finally, they went to the club to see if by a remote chance I was there. When they came in, they saw me dancing with a woman much older than I was. They grabbed me out of there, pulling my ear. They spanked me all the way down to our home and then my father used that belt on me. Never again, I went to that club.

YOUTH PASTIMES

HORTENSIA LÓPEZ: When I was young, we would have lots of family and friends' gatherings. At that time, we had no television. Unfortunately, that device killed the gatherings. At home, after supper was finished, we would remain seated at the table telling stories, playing games and reciting poetry.

We also played "El juego de prendas" ("Game of forfeits"). It was a lot of fun. One of us would be the host and call out a question, pointing at someone around the table. If the person had the wrong answer, he or she, would have to take off a piece of jewelry, be it a ring, a pendant, an earring or any piece of jewelry and put it into a hat. As punishment, he or she would have to recite a poem, kiss somebody on the cheek or eat something not very tasteful. At the end of the game, the person with the most right answers and the most pieces of jewelry collected would be the winner. It was a very sane game and very entertaining.

At those gatherings, we also played and heard music. The Hernández brothers would come to my home to play. Their father was a music teacher and they were very good musicians. Most of the times there was one of the girls at home who played the piano and my brother would play the flute. We listened to music for a couple of hours and everything was finished by ten at the latest.

Sunday afternoons we would go to the park. We would get dressed and go to the park. Those who didn't know us well would walk behind us there. Those who were friends walked side-by-side with us. Once in a while, those who we didn't know would say a *piropo* (compliment). Some of them were very funny.

Later in the evening, the Santiago de Cuba Municipal Band would come out marching around the Hotel Casa Grande and played in the park. Once they finished playing, we would all say goodbye and go home. That was a long time ago.

VÍCTOR VEGA: Many people from Camagüey emigrated to the United States, Mexico and the Dominican Republic during the War of Independence. When the war was over, they returned and settled in the Caridad District.

Among the emigrés, was Doña Ángela del Castillo y Agramonte, who moved right across from us. She had been a very good friend of José Martí and was married to Fernández Ledesma, who had been José Martí's fellow prisoner in 1869 for his political activism against the Spanish.

Fernández Ledesma was much older than Martí and when the latter came to the United States, he helped him a lot. As a matter of fact, the first place he stayed, was at his residence. I know this well because Martí wrote about it in his works and also, because Doña Ángela told me so.

Fernández Ledesma and Doña Ángela had a daughter who would always show us a poem which Martí wrote for her. It was called "Cocola: la tormenta." ("Cocola: The Storm"). It is in one of his children's poetry books. Martí called her by her nickname "Cocola" because her name was Isabel Carolina. Everyone also called her "Cocola." Her husband was an Italian-American named Emilio Passi Cassipapini. He had fought in the Cuban War of Independence in 1895, and he was a hypnotist.

At that time, there was only one theater in town that showed silent movies. They cost five cents for both children and adults and were shown only on Thursdays and Sundays. The theater's name was "El Palco."So, "El Palco," and family gatherings were the only pastimes. At those gatherings, one of the young ladies played the piano and another one recited poetry.

In our neighborhood, there lived Carlos Guerra Agüero who had returned from exile and lived next door to us. There, at his home, Emilio would come and hypnotize Guerra's servants. That show was only for the elders, but we would stand behind the barred windows and peeked to see what was going on in their courtyard. I really would never forget the things I saw. He, for instance, would tell one of the black servants: "You are a rider, c'mon and ride a horse." He would take a *taburete*[28] and order the servant to sit on it and ride it as if it were a horse. The man would be totally hypnotized and ride it.

Afterwards, he would order him to fall in love with one of the servants and as the black servant was falling in love, he said to him: "Now, tell her that Mr. Guerra doesn't want his servants to be falling in love at his home." He would do as he was told because he was totally hypnotized. It seems like I'm watching all of that right now, right in front of my eyes.

RODOLFO SOTOLONGO: One thing that was amazing for us was the magic lantern. It was sort of like an early movie projector. It used photos on a sheet of glass and there was a lens at the front of the device. A kerosene lamp was the only instrument used to project the images onto a large canvas.

The guy who handled the magic lantern was a Catalonian[29] and his wife helped him by fanning the device with a piece of cardboard so that the lens would not overheat. Since there was no electricity in town, the kerosene lamp was the only light that was used to project the images.

CARLOS MONTERO: One of the favorite pastimes in Cuba was cockfighting. Cockfights were on Sundays or holidays. Colonel Mendieta[30], for example raised gamecocks. He had a farm where he only raised gamecocks. He loved to be in that small farm in

---

[28] Type of chair with no arms used by peasants in Cuba since the sixteenth century. It's made out of wood with leather or goatskin in the seat and back.

[29] From Catalonia, a region in the northeast corner of Spain.

[30] Carlos Mendieta y Montefur (1873-1960). Colonel of the Cuban Liberation Army. He was also a member of the Cuban House of Representatives and leader of the Nationalist Party. He became president of Cuba from January 18, 1934, until his resignation on December 10, 1935. Born in Vueltas, Las Villas Province, on November 13, 1876, he died in Havana, on September 27, 1960.

Bauta, Havana Province. He sure loved that farm. Monteagudo[31] also had some very good gamecocks. Cockfighting took place at the cockpit. There were those who came to see the gamecocks' weigh in and the placing of the steel or sharp tortoise shell spurs on the back of their legs. Later on, at the cockpit, they bet every cent they had.

Cubans love to gamble, so, people played *bolita*[32]. Even our cook would take a quarter, which was what we gave her for transportation, to go out and play *bolita*.

CEFERINO GARCÍA: The only form of entertainment I had was playing dominoes. I learned to play it from watching others, because it was played, practically, at every home. It was the only game I knew. After playing dominoes, I would take a stroll around the park or go to the Casino Español, our social club, or the *Liceo* (another social club). But, at 10 o'clock in the evening, I would go home because I had to get up at six in the morning the next day.

When I was young, the word rest didn't exist because grocery stores had to open very early. However, at times, the Spanish would go on outings. I get very emotional remembering those outings. One day, I asked someone to make a cooler out of an old 50-gallon kerosene drum we had, so we could put beer, wine, water, and refreshments for the outings. Since I was in charge of making the list of those who were coming, as well as the food and drinks, I had to make sure we had enough.

On our outings we would eat roast goat or roast pork. Generally, we would go by the river dam or the Begoña Farm. I remember some of the guys that went on those outings such as Nardo Gil or "Pancho," who used to work at the Cuban Electric Com-

---

[31] José de Jesús Monteaguado. General of the Cuban Liberation Army and Commander of Cuba's Rural Guard in 1908, during the second American occupation of the island. He became Cuban Army Chief of Staff in 1912.

[32] An illicit gambling game very popular in Cuba during the nineteenth and twentieth centuries. In *bolita* people placed bets on numbers from 1 to 100. Although it was prohibited, authorities rarely enforced the ban.

pany. Generally, about eight of us would go on the outings and we always divided the costs among ourselves. One of us was a baker, so the bread was free. They were buns. They were made out of flour and pure lard. Everybody loved them. In those outings, all we did was to tell stories, and gossip a bit. We also talked about our businesses. Often, we would talk about getting rich. Some made it, while others, unfortunately, did not.

RICARDO COBIÁN: It was usual to go to the park on Sundays. The park was the place where young people went, but by ten in the evening, everyone went home. On Sundays, everyone tried to be well-dressed. Everyone had their Sunday dress or suit. They were of the best quality that they could be.

ENRIQUE CASERO: We used to go to watch silent movies at the Heredia Theater. We used to buy potato chips and eat them while we were watching the movies. They were silent movies. At the stage corner, there was a guy playing the drums to make the whole thing more exciting or to add suspense to it. For example, when the movie showed actors riding horses, he would take a pair of dry coconut shells and pound them on a surface to sound like the horse trotting. In Cuba, at that time, there were neither fans nor air-conditioners so we would use hand fans at those movies.

CELESTINO SUÁREZ: We young ones did a lot of things. We went out to play pool or dominoes once or twice a week. The thing we did a lot was to watch baseball games. There were all kinds of baseball clubs and we, in Cienfuegos, had some very good players.

At times, teams from Santa Clara or Sagua, would come to play in Cienfuegos and at times our club would go to either city. The fans from those cities would await for our train to be reaching the station so they could throw rocks at the train. However, we used to do the same thing as they did. We also would go to the market to pick up rotten eggs and throw them at our opponents.

Baseball was taken very seriously in Cuba. One time, Cienfuegos brought an American player who played in the Negro

Leagues in the United States, in order to help the team. One day, the poor man missed catching a fly ball and our team lost. They had to escort him out of the ballpark. There were about 20 to 30 police officers escorting him because the fans said he had "sold out" and wanted to kill him.

During my times, there were excellent baseball players. There was Méndez[33], who beat the Americans. Also, there were Miguel Ángel González[34], Aldolfo Luque[35], and Conrado Marrero[36]. There was another player who became famous who played all positions, but I can't remember his name.

We also liked boxing very much. There was a boxer named Quintana[37] who came to the United States and won a match. There was also Vila[38], a promoter who brought foreign boxers to Cuba.

---

[33] José Méndez (1887-1929). Known as "the Black Diamond," Méndez was a famous Cuban pitcher who beat several American pitching stars when their team played exhibition games in Cuba. Méndez also pitched with the Kansas City Monarchs in the Negro Leagues of the United States. He was born in Cárdenas, Matanzas Province, on September 3, 1887, and died in Havana, on October 31, 1929.

[34] Miguel Ángel González (1890-1977). One of the first Cuban players to play in the Major Leagues. González, a catcher, played with several teams and briefly managed the St. Louis Cardinals. He was born in Havana on September 24, 1890, and died there on February 19, 1977.

[35] Adolfo Luque (1890-1957). One of the first Cuban players to play in the Major Leagues. Luque, a pitcher, played mostly with the Cincinnati Reds. During his 21 year career in the Majors he won 194 games. He was born in Havana, on August 4, 1890, and died in said city, on July 3, 1957.

[36] Conrado Marrero (1911-2014). Known as "El Premier," Marrero did not play in the Major Leagues until he was 38 years old. He played for the perennial cellar-dwellers Washington Senators from 1950 until 1954, winning 39 games. He was born in Laberinto, a farm near Sagua la Grande, Las Villas Province, on April 25, 1911, and died in Havana, on April 23, 2014.

[37] Known as "the Cuban Lion," Eliseo Quintana was one of the best middleweight boxers of the 1920s. He compiled a 42-13-6 record as a boxer.

[38] A former light heavyweight boxer of the 1930s, Vila became a manager and promoter. As a promoter, he was known for bringing American boxers to Cuba.

One day, promoters brought a black heavyweight champion[39] to Cuba to fight a guy called "the White Hope." This black was married to a French white woman. It seems that Americans didn't like that, and they made Havana the match venue. So, the Americans, who controlled the boxing world, told the black guy that he would have to "throw" the match, otherwise, they would kill him. Well, he "threw" the match, because, otherwise they were going to kill him.

MANUEL GARCÍA IGLESIAS: Generally, everyone dressed very well on Sundays. That is to say, the guy who had his best suit, wore it at Sunday Mass or at other places.Going to the park on Sunday was a great pasttime. Strolling there in the late afternoon or the evening was a big thing. Either at Libertad Park or Independencia Park, there were concerts. People would stroll in circles, women would stroll one way, and men would stroll the other way, so they would always face one another.

There were also lots of wooden benches placed around the gazebo. There were wrought iron chairs for rent. During my youth, the one who rented the chairs was Mr. Stacholy. He would charge five cents for the chairs and ten cents for the rocking chairs. On a given Sunday, one could be sitting there from seven in the evening making flirtatious *piropos* to the women passing by. I think the *piropo* tradition came from the Spanish. Some of the *piropos* were the usual ones like "you are beautiful" or "you are the prettiest creature in the world." However, there were others that were a bit unrefined like "If you cook the way you walk, I would eat the sticky crust at the bottom of the rice bowl." These *piropos* were not to be offensive, but rather complimentary of women.

---

[39] The heavyweight championship match took place on April 5, 1915, in Havana, Cuba, between champion Jack Johnson, the first African-American heavyweight boxing champion and white challenger Jess Willard. Johnson was knocked out in the twenty-sixth round. According to Johnson, he "threw" the fight because of death threats. Throughout his career, Johnson had received death threats for marrying a white woman.

GRACIELA DUBROCQ: For the young ladies of Matanzas, dances were their favorite. Once a month, there was a dance at the Matanzas *Liceo*. Young girls who were less than 15 years old, could attend but weren't allowed to dance because they were considered minors. Pepe Quirós would take us to those dances. He was a great music teacher. We would just sit there and watch people dance. To attend these dances, we would wear tea length dresses. We were all dressed up because that was pretty much the code.

We also attended concerts in the park. There were two music bands. One was the Municipal Band and the other was the Army Regiment Band. My brother played with the Municipal Band. There, in Matanzas, we had two concerts per week.

Regarding dances, the music piece that was the most played was the *danzón*. To me, the *danzón* is one of the most beautiful musical compositions because it has many parts. The first part is always repeated until the end. The *danzón* is a *danza* offshoot. The *danza* is originally French. It was brought to Spain later and much later there was the *contra danza*.

There was a black musician in Matanzas named Miguel Failde[40]. This man was a composer who composed music for dances. One day, he composed a piece which he called *danzón*, with a more varied rhythm than the *danza*. He premiered this piece at the Matanzas *Liceo*, in 1879. The first *danzón* he wrote was named "Las Alturas de Simpson" because there is a district in Matanzas named after Mr. Simpson who lived in that area. That district overlooks the city and it's around *La Ermita de Monserrate*[41].

---

[40] Miguel Failde (1852-1921). Cuban musician, creator of the *danzón*, Cuba's national dance. Besides "Las Alturas de Simpson," Failde composed other popular *danzones* such as "Ingratitud" and "Delirio." Failde was born in Guacamaro, Matanzas Provinice, on December 23, 1852, and died in Matanzas, on December 26, 1921.

[41] Famous Cuban chapel built in 1875 by Matanza's Catalonian community. It was built in honor of the Virgin of Montserrat. The Montserrat Monastery is located near Barcelona.

Cuban music is beautiful. I'm always afraid of running out of traditional music for my piano repertoire. I've been playing Cuban music since I was seven years old. I remember when I was seven and they took me to the theater as a child prodigy to play Verdi's "El cuarteto de Rigoleto."[42] When I was right on the stage, I said to myself "why would I want to play 'El cuarteto de Rigoleto,' I better play 'El bombín de Barreto,'[43] and I played it." The audience gave me a standing ovation because I played it without rehearsing it and they noticed it was impromptu. However, the theater's owner came over to me and said, "you've done great, but I'll give you a small present if you play 'El cuarteto de Rigoleto,' because it's on the program." Well, I played it, and he gave me a gold chain and small golden religious medal.

LORENZO ZEQUEIRA: When I was young, I danced a lot. There were many clubs that held dances such as *danzones*, waltzes, and *pasodobles*[44]. There were other places that one could go dancing for a fee. They would give you a card and a small pencil, you would write the piece you wanted for them to play and you would dance with a woman when it was your turn. It was in one of those places where I learned to dance the foxtrot.

I knew many Cuban singers, players and composers such as Cheo Belén Puig[45], Paulina Alvarez[46] and Facundo Rivero[47]. I

---

[42] Musical composition which appears in the third act of Giusseppe Verdi's opera *Rigoletto*

[43] One of the most popular *danzones* in Cuban music. It was composed in 1920 by Cuban composer José Urfé.

[44] Lively Spanish ball dance modeled after the drama of the traditional Spanish bullfight

[45] Cheo Belén Puig (1908-1971). Cuban pianist, composer and *danzón* orchestra conductor. He was born in Havana on December 29, 1908 and died there on May 15, 1971.

[46] Paulina Alvarez (1912-1965). She was known as "The Empress of the *Danzonete,*" a version of the *danzón*, created by the *matancero* composer Aniceto Díaz (1887-1964). She was born in Cienfuegos, Las Villas Province, on June 29, 1912, and died in Havana, on July 22, 1961.

was even president of a group called "Los Jóvenes de Vals" ("The Waltz's Youth").

ENRIQUE CASERO: Whenever I went to a dance in Santiago, I would wear my white linen suit. I also would go to dances in the countryside. The *danzones* were played there a lot and the *contrabajo* which is the big base instrument was used there a lot too. One day, I went to a dance in one of those hamlets. It had rained a lot and there was mud all over the place. The poor musicians had so much trouble carrying the *contrabajo* and lifting it that I said to myself "Damn it, the *contrabajo* bears its name quite well" because in our language "con trabajo" means lots of hassle.

CELESTINO SUÁREZ: In Cienfuegos there were lots of dances. I hardly went to those dances because my father was Spanish and didn't belong to the *Liceo* where they were held. One of the *Liceo's* most important balls was the Queen's Ball. One day there was a lot of grumbling among its members because they were going to crown a queen who wasn't pretty at all. She had been selected not because of her beauty, but because her father had a lot of money.

The *Liceo's* Board of Directors knew that there was a lot of discontent with her selection and were afraid something bad was going to happen. So, they brought in a number of police officers as a security measure. When the Queen's name was announced, all hell broke loose. During the mayhem and all the chaos, the police beat the hell out of the prominent citizens. I think they did it on purpose and said to themselves "This is our opportunity to get even with the haves in town." I remember that event very well, and even today I laugh at what happened there.

---

[47] Facundo Rivero (1910-?). Cuban pianist and founder of the famous Rivera orchestra. He was born in Santa Clara, Las Villas Province, in 1910, and died in Havana

COURTSHIPS OF YESTERYEARS

RODOLFO SOTOLONGO: There were different courtship types. The courtship started with the young man being interested in the young lady. He might have met her at a dance or walking down the street.

A long time ago, young ladies were very reserved, so the young man had to "sell the product.""Selling the product" meant that the young man would walk around the block where the young lady lived several times. If she was interested in him, she would peek through the windows or come out to the front porch. Then, the love letters would follow as a way of communicating between them. Later on, they would see each other by the wrought-iron front window, and that was very much it.

In order for the courtship to materialize, the young man needed to have a future, be it a job, money or anything economically sound. Once the young lady's parents approved the courtship, the "boyfriend" would visit the "girlfriend's" home. He could visit the home as a friend but not as a "boyfriend." That didn't happen until the asking for the hand occured. Asking for her hand happened when the young man's father or parents would visit the young lady's parents to formally ask for her hand on his behalf. If the young lady's parents accepted their request, then the young man could visit the young lady's home, officially as her fiancé.

The parents would set up the visitation hours which were always in the evening, but the fiancé couldn't stay for long. While he visited her, they would sit vis-à-vis on a pair of rocking chairs and the mother would sit nearby watching them. If they wanted to go out on a date, they couldn't go out alone; the mother had to go with them. Often, the aunts and sisters would also go and the poor guy would be escorted by a family squadron.

JOSEFINA PÉREZ: There were couples who were married after a short courtship and those who were married after a long one. I had a friend who had a twenty-year courtship and finally got married.

There were different types of courtship. There were parents who were opposed to the courtship and they would not allow the young man in their home. Therefore, he would have to see her outside, on the street, in front of the living room wrought-iron window and talk to her right there. If she noticed that someone was approaching, she would whisper: "Leave, get out, someone is coming." He would leave right away, and she would remain there, faking as if she were looking at people passing by. At times, they continued to persist in their courtship, but at other times, when there was so much family opposition, they simply had to break up.

The young man who was accepted at the young lady's home would visit her every night. He would remove his straw hat and sit close to the door. The young lady and the young man would sit facing each other. There was always a family member watching them because they were never allowed to be unsupervised.

If everything was approved, the asking for her hand was next. The young man's father or one of his family members would go to meet the young lady's parents. This person would summarize the young man's great qualities and ask for the young lady's hand. If her parents approved, they would get married. If the bride's parents were rich, they would give the couple a dowry. The bride's family would be responsible for the wedding expenses and the groom's family for the household expenses.

Many of the weddings during my times, were officiated right at the bride's home. The priest would come and marry the couple right at an altar built by the bride's family at the home.

CARLOS MONTERO: There were different types of courtship. There was the window courtship and the home courtship. There were also those in which there were financial difficulties at the young lady's home. Therefore, what her family wanted was for her to marry someone who was well off in order to solve their economic woes.

If a young man was poor or broke, he might as well be struck by lightning, because he could never marry the young lady. Of course, there was also the scoundrel who would try to sneak a couple of kisses through the window while nobody was watching.

Today, making out and that type of thing is very common. During my times, a young lady going out with a young man by themselves was unacceptable. They had to go out with the mother, the aunt, or another family member. Nowadays, things are different, but that's the way it is.

HORTENSIA LÓPEZ: I don't know about courtship in other families, but in mine, my mother was very strict and my father was even stricter. There was a young guy who was fond of me, but my father didn't like him because he didn't consider him fit to be my husband. So I will tell you how it ended.

I remember that he lived across the street and one day, he came to visit me and gave me a lightning bug. My sister, Elvirita, was crazy about the lightning bug. At that time we had two huge hutches where we kept our dinnerware and glassware. I took away the lightning bug and placed it inside a glass cup, so that later its light would shine at night. However, my sister saw me doing that and tried climbing the hutch to retrieve the lightning bug, but when she got to the top, the whole thing came crashing down and everyone heard the horrible noise. Fortunately, nothing happened to my sister, but everything was broken into different pieces. Then, the guy who had a crush on me and was sort of a poet, wrote a poem that went like this:

> To the cute señorita
> The beautiful Hortensita
> I wasn't allowed to give her a hug
> So, I gave her a lightning bug
> She placed it on top of the hutch
> Right inside a glass cup
> But as Elvirita tried to climb the hutch
> To get the lightning bug

> The whole hutch came crashing down
> In disbelief, I turned around
> Only to see my world turned upside down.

Needless to say, that was the last time he set foot on our home. My father was mad, really mad, I never saw him so mad.

There was also the letter courtship. I had a friend who was very nice. One day, he brought me some magazines. When I went to look for them, I couldn't find them. I asked my mother if she knew where they were. She told me: "They are in the trash can." I said to her that he had told me that there was something important inside one of them. She replied: "Yes, there was something inside. It was a love letter and I kept it." My mother was something else. She watched us like a hawk.

**Hortensia López, 1983
(Courtesy of Frank Fernández)**

CELESTINO SUÁREZ: My mother worried about our household servants just like she worried about us. They were single women around 20 and they began to have boyfriends. The young man would come to the window to see one of them. My mother would come out and tell him: "If you are a man with good intentions, you don't have to be standing on the street. If you want to marry her, just come in."

There were three household servants at different times in my home and the three of them got married. They were named Vicenta, Ana and Victoria. As a matter of fact, my father walked them down the aisle.

MARÍA ELBA GONZÁLEZ: During Spanish colonial times there were pre-arranged marriages between families. For example, my grandmother married the man that her father chose for her. It didn't matter. It was "Do as I tell you." However, my generation had more freedom, for we had the right to choose.

BAPTISMS, WAKES AND EULOGIES

RODOLFO SOTOLONGO: Baptisms were always conducted at church on Sundays. A baptism was a big thing for kids. When the bells began ringing, we would know that the ceremony was over. We would quickly run over to the church entrance because it was customary for the *padrino* (godfather) to toss coins to the kids waiting at the church entrance. When the *padrino* came out of the church we would yell: "*Padrinito*, throw me a *realito*.[48]" He would toss coins and we would pile up, trying to pick up the coins.

JOSEFINA PÉREZ: A baptism was a big feast in our town. The family would go to the cathedral to baptize the child and later they would come home where there was a big party with all of the expenses paid by the godparents. Over there, it was customary when a child was baptized, the godparents had to pay for everything. Once a child was baptized, the godparents became responsible for the child's welfare in case the parents died.

FELIPE ROLOFF: In the countryside, the overwhelming majority of baptisms were on *Sábado de Gloria*[49]. Announcements would go out throughout the area, indicating the baptisms' time

---

[48] Spanish diminutive for a *real*, a Cuban coin worth ten cents.

[49] Easter Saturday also known as Holy Saturday or Great Sabbath. In early Christianity it was customary to baptize those who wanted to become Christians during that Saturday evening. On November 19, 1955, Pope Pius XII's liturgical reform ended the term Easter Saturday, and replaced it with the term Holy Saturday. While Easter Saturday was a day of festivities, Holy Saturday became a day of recollection. However, in the Cuban countryside, the festivity tradition of *Sabado Santo* continued until the Cuban Revolution put an end to religious ceremonies.

and place, followed by a horseback riding tournament and dance.

The priest would come from Morón on horseback because there was no other form of transportation. I remember that at times there were over 200 baptisms on a single *Sábado de Gloria* around our area. They were mass baptisms. I remember the children crying when holy water was poured on their foreheads and the godparents standing beside their particular godchild.

It was an honor to be a godfather or a godmother. To become a *compadre* or a *comadre* was something sacred. If the *compadres* were not family members; they had to be the parents' best friends or those who were very important to them. It was an extraordinary honor to be godparents.

JOSEFINA PÉREZ: When I was a child, wakes would take place at the deceased's home because there were no funeral homes in Cienfuegos. While the wake was going on, the family would set a table in the dining room full of tidbits like crackers, olives and other things. If it was in winter they would serve hot chocolate. Later on, when there were funeral homes, wakes were conducted in those places, and no food was provided.

FELIPE ROLOFF: Wakes in the countryside were very interesting. When someone died, several people from the area would go on horseback to tell others that so-and-so had died, and people would come to the deceased's home.

If it was early in the morning, the family would slaughter a pig or chickens so that people attending the wake would have something to eat. One has to realize that there were people that had traveled a long distance just to be with the family and had to stay there until the next day when the burial would take place.

Before the funeral procession departed, breakfast, consisting of coffee, milk, bread, butter, cheese and crackers would be served. Afterwards, the funeral procession would depart for the particular town's cemetery. Generally, the cemetery was quite a distance away. In those places, a long litter would be built and that was where the wooden coffin was placed. Four people would carry the litter for a distance of about a *cordel*[50] or two, and then four others would relieve them.

There were funeral processions that were really big with 400 or 500 people on horseback. If it was in the spring, it was something terrible because of the rain and the mud. Coffins were made out of wood with cloth covering the inside and there was always a crucifix on the coffin's top. Funeral costs were inexpensive because there was a lot of wood in the area.

RODOLFO SOTOLONGO: The wake took place at the deceased's home. In the evening, coffee was served and at times food. To transport the coffin, there was a horse-drawn hearse and the horses would have black harnesses. A coachman dressed in black with a top hat would drive the hearse, and the procession would follow on foot. The procession would stop at the cemetery and someone would deliver the eulogy.

I remember one occasion when a widow died. She was a very difficult person and didn't get along with anyone. She didn't have any friends in town and no family. The day of the wake not a single person attended it.

The day of the funeral there was no one to deliver the eulogy, and the town's mayor took it upon himself to deliver it. He asked a group of neighbors to come to the funeral procession as a goodwill gesture. Some attended against their own will because the woman had been very mean; however, they attended as a favor to the mayor.

When it was time for him to deliver the eulogy, the mayor didn't know what to say. He couldn't talk about her kindness or friendship. He couldn't say anything good because she was hated. However, just as the coffin was about to be lowered into the ground, a storm full of rain, lightning and thunder started and since

---

[50] Cuban agrarian measure equivalent to 20 meters in length.

her name was Soledad[51], the mayor who was very witty, realizing that thunder and lightning had just started, delivered a very short eulogy by saying: "Ladies and gentlemen, Soledad has just arrived in heaven."

MANUEL GARCÍA IGLESIAS: *Velorios* (wakes) were held in the deceased's home. There were no such things as funeral homes. A wake would last the whole night until the following morning. It was customary to serve coffee, hot chocolate, sweets and pastries.

When I was a young man, a group of guys founded the "Sagua Velorio Club" in order to attend as many wakes as they could, so that they could take advantage of what was being served. One day, one of them forgot that he had placed a small alarm clock in his pocket and the alarm started ringing as he was viewing the deceased in the coffin. Embarrassed, they all took off running.

Another time, there was a Chinese lottery vendor. The poor man was assaulted and assassinated, so the Chinese community held a wake for him. The Chinese were known to serve plenty of food at their wakes and they would also serve hard liquor. So, all of the guys went to the wake and got drunk. One of them, Rául, nicknamed "Guanajera" ("Tukey") took a piece of guava paste with cheese, went to the coffin and said: "This poor man, no one has fed him. I'm going to feed him." He took the guava paste and the cheese and placed it in the deceased's mouth. Naturally, the Chinese took offense and went after them with knives. The guys ran away at full speed with the Chinese running after them. I remember they took refuge at the "Hotel Unión." It was a miracle that they escaped with their lives.

---

[51] Name given to a female in honor of Our Lady of Solitude.

CHRISTMAS AND HOLY WEEK

MARIA ELBA GONZÁLEZ: The *Nochebuena* (Christmas Eve) was celebrated at home. All the family gathered around the table to eat roast pork, guinea hen, and all kinds of nougat. At around ten in the evening, everyone would leave to see Christmas decorations made by the San Salvador and Carmen districts. The two districts were rivals and competed with each other as to which one had the best decorations around the town's square. At the start of the Christmas season, the rich families donated money for the lights and other decorations.

On December 8, people from each district would go around town with their cowbells and tin cans collecting money for their decorations. I remember one night that one of those districts built a huge log pyramid for a bonfire right in front of the *Casino Español*. It was so huge that it was seen even in Santa Clara. It lit the whole town of Remedios and at the same time there were fireworks.

There was such a rivalry between the two districts. The ones from Carmen would say: "Get out of the way, San Salvador, get out of the way." The ones from San Salvador would say: "Where are you going San Salvador on such a dark evening? I'm going to dig a grave because Carmen is dead and gone, dead and gone." The rivalry was so deep that families from one district would not say hello to the ones from the other district until January 1, when everything ended.

A few days later on January 6, *Los Tres Reyes Magos* (The Three Wise Men) would come to bring gifts to the children. If they behaved well during the year they got a lot of toys but if they misbehaved they got charcoal. Kids would write letters asking for the gifts they wanted The Three Wise Men to bring them, and place them inside their shoes. When they awoke, the gifts were there and they were very happy.

CELESTINO SUÁREZ: Christmas Eve was celebrated on the 24th, but since my father was a butcher and had a lot of work that day, we celebrated Christmas afternoon. We had black beans, yucca, roast pork, cider, wine and for dessert, we had Spanish nougats.

I don't remember having a Christmas tree at home, but we had a Nativity scene. I remember that at our Jesuit school we sang a Christmas Carol that went like this:

> Eager shepherds
> On our way to Bethlehem
> We are going to see
> The newly born King
> We are going to see our Emmanuel
> Let us bring flowers, nougat and honey
> We are going to see
> The newly born King
> We are going to see our Emmanuel.

ANA AURORA RECIO: My father was a *Nochebuena* enthusiast. Four days before *Nochebuena*, he would go out to make preparations. That evening, we would have between eighty-two to a hundred people sitting at the table, eating roast pork, and turkey brought from our farm. We also had pheasant which my father liked a lot. We did not celebrate Christmas or New Year's Eve; just *Nochebuena*.

MANUEL GARCÍA IGLESIAS: Roast pork on *Nochebuena* was indispensable. We would make a hole in the ground and filled it with charcoal. We would have four cinderblocks and some iron rods a few inches above the hole with the cinderblocks holding the rods. Then, we placed the dressed pig and roasted it for a few hours. So, we ate roast pork, black beans and rice, lettuce and radish salad, nougat, and quince.

Afterwards, we would go to Midnight Mass. Next day, Christmas Day, we would only eat *montería*, a dish made out of pork leftovers with olives, potatoes and lots of condiment which we added to it. We would not eat that meal until two or three in the afternoon because we were so full from eating so much the previous evening.

JOSEFINA PÉREZ: Holy Week was a much-respected week. In those days, floors were swept on Maundy Thursday so they didn't have to be swept on Good Friday. People said that if someone swept on Good Friday, he or she would incur God's wrath. It was said that on Good Friday, the devil was on the loose. I don't know whether those things were true or not, but I followed them.

FELIPE ROLOFF: No one worked after Maundy Thursday. On Maundy Thursday at noon, cane cutting stopped and the sugar mills also stopped their grinding. On Good Friday, for example, people were accustomed to going fishing in the river. There was good fishing where I lived and that day everyone ate fish. For us, Holy Week ended on *Sábado Santo* and that was when baptisms, tournaments and dances were celebrated. Holy Week was one of the great Cuban traditions, but here, it's hardly respected.

RODOLFO SOTOLONGO: Holy Week was observed in absolute silence. There were no parties and the town was calm. All of the sacred statues and images at church were draped. On Thursday, Father Manuel would wash the feet of 12 children with holy water. That tradition is still going on because I've seen the Pope on television washing the feet of 12 people at the Vatican.

ANA AURORA RECIO: In Camagüey, during Holy Week, there was the Holy Sepulcher Procession. It was something marvelous to see that piece of work The Holy Sepulcher was made out of silver. A rich man in town paid for it. This man had two sons. One was his own son and the other was adopted. Somehow, perhaps because of jealousy, the adopted one killed his brother. Although this happened during Spanish colonial times, the rich man, a Cuban, had this great artwork built in memory of his son. I can't remember his name[52], for it was a long time ago.

MARÍA ELBA GONZÁLEZ: We had lots of traditions in Remedios. One of the main ones and the one we really loved was Holy Week. That week started with Palm Sunday, when palm fronds and leaves blessed with holy water were distributed at church.

Following Palm Sunday, processions were held throughout the week. Several people in town would build the Stations of the Cross right outside their living room window and the procession would stop at each station.

One of the most important processions was the one on Maundy Thursday. They would bring out a statue of Jesus the Nazarene followed by the one of our Lady of Sorrows[53] with the seven swords piercing her heart. My grandmother used to make the dresses for that statue. They were beautiful! Both, the dress and the veil were made out of the finest cloth, embroidered with the finest golden thread.

On Good Friday, there was the Holy Sepulcher Procession which was the largest in town. In Remedios, the women used to dress in black. Each woman would wear her Spanish silk veil and her *peineta* (high comb). Those in the procession, accompanied a sepulcher made out of silver and crystal with the statue of the dead Jesus inside. The sepulcher should still be at the church unless the Communists have stolen it. In this procession, only the statue of

---

[52] According to the legend, the man was named Manuel de la Virgen Agüero. It's a fact that the Holy Sepulcher was finished in 1762.

[53] One of the names given to the *Mater Dolorosa*. The seven swords represent the events in the life of the Blessed Virgin Mary. The following are the events: The Prophecy of Simeon, the Escape and Flight to Egypt, the Loss of the Child Jesus in the Temple, the Meeting of Mary and Jesus on the Via Dolorosa, the Crucifixion of Jesus on Mount Calvary, the Piercing of the Side of Jesus and His Descent from the Cross and the Burial of Jesus.

Our Lady of Solitude[54] accompanied the statue of the dead Jesus. The statue of Our Lady of Solitude belonged to my family. It was a marvelous one and Our Lady's face was beautiful. Our family donated the statue to the church when we left Cuba.

Once the procession turned around the street, the Holy Sepulcher was returned to the church; everyone entered the church to listen to the Sermon of the Solitude. There was a magnificent priest whose last name was Ortiz. They always brought him to preach the sermon.

On Easter Sunday, Jesus's statue would be brought out of the church, through the main door, and a procession would start marching around the park. Then, through a side door, the John the Apostle statue would come out in another procession and linked with the main procession. The Saint John's Procession would return to the church to meet the Our Lady of Sorrow's statue and bring her the good news that her son had resurrected. Afterwards, the procession carrying Jesus's statue would return to the church through the main door and Easter Mass would be celebrated.

However, things were not over. There were all kinds of Judas's figures hanging from the park lampposts. So, after the Mass, people began burning them. It was something else seeing this spectacle. I will never forget it.

---

[54] Another representation of the *Mater Dolorosa* in solitude contemplating the death of her son. The statue is dressed in black and white and her hands are clasped.

FEAST DAYS, HOLIDAYS, AND CARNIVALS

VÍCTOR VEGA CEBALLOS: In Camagüey we celebrated the feast days of several saints, but the most important one was *La Caridad*[55]. The events leading to the feast day started around the first days in September. The mayor would go to *La Caridad* Church, climb the church tower and raise the Cuban flag. Later on, he would give a speech and announce the different activities taking place. There were numerous activities because the feast would last until September 12.

There were a number of kiosks and stands selling sodas, candy, fruit, cookies and other goodies. However, the most important feature was the feast day's religious tone. The two most important days were *La Caridad* Feast Day on September 8 and the festival's closing on September 12.

On September 8, at the crack of dawn a Mass was celebrated. People would come down from all parts of the city, even the most remote ones. I used to see people coming down from the bridge and those who had made a promise to Our Lady, in order to obtain her graces, would remove their shoes and walk barefoot the rest of the way in fulfillment of their promise.

There were others who walked on their knees for more than a kilometer until they reached the church. Once they reached the church, they would climb the stairs, walk all the way to the altar, kiss *La Caridad's* statue, make the sign of the cross and stand

---

[55] Our Lady of Charity, known throughout Cuba as *La Caridad del Cobre*. According to the story, in 1612, three men named Juan, two of them Indians and one black set out for Nipe Bay, on their open boat to transport salt to the town of El Cobre near Santiago de Cuba. A huge storm caught them and were about to perish when the Our Lady's image appeared and rescued them. The statue of Our Lady has been venerated in Cuba ever since. In 1916, Our Lady of Charity, was declared patroness of Cuba by Pope Benedict XV.

up. Many of those had their knees covered with blood. I also saw people on their knees, walking with a pair of bricks in their hands.

I always accompanied my mother to that Mass. There was a black lady who lived around the church in a rundown wooden house full of holes. That poor woman washed and ironed clothes for a living and her name was María Sánchez. When we used to go by her home, we would see the daylight coming through the wood holes. My mother would approach those holes and say: "Good morning, María Sánchez." Although she couldn't see my mother, she would recognize her voice and would reply: "Good morning, Luisa Ceballos; may God grant you a peaceful day."

HORTENSIA LÓPEZ: The most important holiday in Santiago was New Year's Eve. People would go to the San Carlos Hotel and wait until midnight for the raising of the Cuban flag and the playing of the national anthem. As they were raising the flag, we would watch from the balcony. It was a beautiful flag donated by Emilio Bacardí[56]. If the flag waved a lot, people said it was going to be a good year, full of prosperity and happiness. If the flag was still, people said it was going to be a bad year.

RODOLFO SOTOLONGO: The most important feast day in Colón was Saint Joseph's which is March 19. St. Joseph was Colón's patron saint. That day, people decorated their porches with royal palm tree fronds. Later, in the afternoon, a procession would come out of the church and go around town. The ladies, dressed in white, would hold candles in their hand and the men followed them. We would walk all of Diego Street, turn on Cervantes Street, all the way to Real Street until reaching Isabel Segunda Street.

---

[56] Emilio Bacardí y Moreau (1844 -1922). Colonel in Cuban Liberation Army, mayor of Santiago de Cuba (1901- 1905), and Oriente Province senator. He was one of the most respected historians of the Cuban War of Independence. Author of *Doña Guiomar*, a historical novel, he was also an executive in the family's Bacardí Distilling Company. He was born in Santiago de Cuba on June 5, 1844, and died in that city, in 1922.

That day was a special day. There were cockfights and tournaments. In those days, tournaments consisted of riders showing their skills. They would ride their horses and their horses' neck hair would be twisted with laces all over. A rope with many rings was tied from one post to the other on the street. Each rider - carrying a lance - with the horse galloping at full speed had to hook the ring with his lance. There were two teams. One was the blue team and the other one was the red team. Every time a rider hooked a ring, a young lady selected as the team's princess gave the rider a ribbon. At the tournament's end, the team with the most ribbons collected was the winner.

MARÍA ELBA CONZÁLEZ: My town's official name was San Juan de los Remedios. That day, all of the peasants from the countryside would come to town on horseback to celebrate Saint John the Baptist's Feast Day, which is on June 24. There were many events that day. One of the events involved kids riding bicycles trying to hook rings tied to a rope. Another event was the greasy pole climbing. There were all kinds of entertainment for everyone. Later on, in the evening, different social clubs sponsored dinners and dances and people enjoyed themselves tremendously.

There was an interesting tradition in town. On Saint John's Feast Day Eve, young ladies who were single would place a peeled lemon and a whole lemon under their beds. In the morning, on Saint John's Feast Day, they would get up, reach under the bed and pick up one of the lemons. If the whole lemon was picked, it meant that she was going to marry a rich man, but if she picked the peeled one, that meant she was going to marry a poor man.

There was also another tradition and that was placing two bowls under the bed, one containing water and the other containing dirt. In the morning, if she reached under the bed and touched water, it meant that she was going to travel a lot, but if she touched dirt, it meant that she was going to stay in town for the rest of her life. I was very fortunate to see all these events and experience the traditions.

FELIPE ROLOFF: In Cuba, there were many patriotic holidays. In some towns, some of these holidays were more meaningful to the particular town than to others. It all depended on the date. For example, in Bayamo[57], Oriente Province, October 10, was something else. The same happened in Baire[58], Oriente Province, on February 24.

In my home, May 20 was special because it was Cuban Independence Day and my father was a *Mambí*. Additionally, my sister was born on that day. During those days, saints' feast days were celebrated more frequently than birthdays. However, in my home, May 20 was something special because it was an honor for a *Mambí* to have a daughter born on Cuban Independence Day.

**Felipe Roloff, 2007
(Courtesy of Alina Van Tassel)**

---

[57] Cuban city in Oriente Province, where the Cuban uprising against Spanish rule occurred nearby, on October 10, 1868. The event, known as the "Yara Battlecry," started the Ten Years' War of Cuban Independence from 1868 until 1878.

[58] Town in Oriente Province where the "Baire Battlecry," starting the Cuban War of Independence occurred on February 24, 1895.

CARLOS MONTERO: I remember the festivals that took place in Havana's different districts. They were very popular and people would go dancing continuously until dawn. One would go reveling from one district to the other. I remember going from the Jesús del Monte District to the Calabazar de Sagua District on horseback. People would also go by horse carriage. I knew a guy named Felipe, who, by the way, had a brother who was a *bolita* dealer. Well, he had a horse carriage business. My friends and I would ride on those carriages from one place to the other for a few *pesos*. At times, in those districts, someone would get drunk and get punched by someone else, but there was no trouble and shots were never fired.

HORTENSIA LÓPEZ: In Spanish colonial times, when I lived in El Caney, I used to see the *tumbas francesas* coming down from the hills. They had huge drums and the female *tumba francesa* members always wore headbands and multicolored dresses. It would take three days to come down from the hills to El Caney. Once they passed through El Caney, they would later go to a place behind Santiago de Cuba's cemetery. They would spend nights playing the drums, singing and dancing. I would never forget those black ladies with their baggy dresses, smoking cigars while dancing to the drumbeat. The revelry lasted three or four days and when it was over, they returned to the hills.

ENRIQUE CASERO: The Santiago carnival was the most famous in Cuba. One time, there was such a long line of revelers dancing that it went all the way from the Plaza de Armas down to San Pedro Street, turning on to Habana Street, right in front of my home. That was the biggest carnival ever in Santiago.

MARIO VEGA: Santiago de Cuba's carnival was very famous. Garzón Avenue would be closed so that people could come down dancing. Long lines of revelers, four or five blocks long would come down dancing. Along that Avenue, there were all kinds of stalls selling roast pork, black beans, rice and casabe[59].

In Santiago, people drank a lot of beer. The beer brewed in Santiago was the strongest of all Cuban beers. I would drink two bottles of that beer and get woozy. However, a *santiaguero*[60] drank from morning to dark and nothing would happen to him. The *santiaguero* also added Bacardí rum to his coffee.

HORTENSIA LÓPEZ: In Santiago there were many *comparsas*[61]. Each *comparsa* would select a *madrina* (sponsor). On Carnival's day, *comparsas* would come to different homes in the morning asking for donations to give to its *madrina*. At times, they would give her a gold pendant or roses and the *comparsa* would go dancing by her home greeting her. Everything was so colorful, so nice. The bad things that we see today never happened there.

---

[59] Type of bread made out of cassava, very popular in Camagüey and Oriente Provinces.

[60] Person from Santiago de Cuba

[61] A group of street dancers in Cuban carnival processions.

MY HOMETOWN MEMORABLE FOLK CHARACTERS

GRACIELA DUBROCQ: In Matanzas, there was a guy named "Marín chiquito" ("Little Marín"). He was sort of like a messenger boy and used his bicycle to go from place to place. I remember giving him a nickel to go and get something from my grandmother's home. He would get on that bike and would bring it in practically no time at all.

There was another character called "Bayoneta" ("Bayonet"). She was black and was half crazy. People would go to her and tell her: "Bayoneta, you don't have anything down there." She would reply: "What do you mean that I don't have anything down there?" She would then pull up her skirt and yell: "Here, so that you can see I have something down there."

ENRIQUE CASERO: In Santiago there was a character called "Aguacero." ("Rainshower"). Every time one saw him, one would extend his hand, feigning as if it were about to rain, and he would yell: "I'm going to get you, you son-of-a-bitch." There was also another one called "Pisa Bonito" ("Gentle Stepper"). He was a very entertaining guy. He had been a barber at the Borgita sugar mill, near our farm. His shoes were always shining and while he was walking, he used to take off his hat and bow his head every time he met a woman.

JOSEFINA PÉREZ: In Cienfuegos, there was a cart driver nicknamed "Molleja" ("Gizzard") because he was very ugly and had a huge mouth extending from one end to the other. He was always driving his mule cart. There was another one called "Don Domingo, El Aguador." ("Don Domingo, the Water Carrier"). He had a mule cart full of water barrels. Since there was little water in town, one would summon him and he will sell you a water barrel. Another character was "El Manguero" ("The Mango Vendor"). He would go all over Lamar Street crying out loud: "Mangoes for sale." I've never heard someone with such a loud voice.

Perhaps, the most colorful character was "Chito Corúa" ("Chito, the Cormoran"). He was a short mulatto who would always accompany the funeral hearse. He never missed a funeral procession. So, when there was someone who wanted to be everywhere, people would say to him or her: "Hey, you are like "Chito Corúa," going to every funeral procession."

MANUEL GARCÍA: I remember some of the folk characters in my hometown. For example, there was a mentally deranged character nicknamed "Octavio, el Melodioso" ("Octavio, the Melodious One"). He would dance everywhere claiming to be a champion dancer. He was always well-dressed and his suit was full of medals. People would give him fake medals and tell him: "the Spanish King is giving you this medal and the English Prince is giving you this one." He would put them on his suit and go around showing the medals to everyone. There was another character known as "Joaquinito el enano." ("Joaquinito, the Midget"). He was a midget who was always wearing little boys' shorts. He was a 50 or 60 year old guy still wearing his shorts.

Another character was "Ciriaco." We called him "Ciriaco," but I can't repeat the rest of the nickname because it's a very dirty word. He used to push a cart loaded with many things. He pushed it by hand. He was a strong guy.

One colorful character was nicknamed "Cadera el loco" ("The crazy hip hopper"). He was crazy and was always drunk. He was always yelling insults at city officials and other politicians. One day, he went to the marketplace and saw they there were making meat fritters and noticed politicians around the stand eating them. He looked right at them and started yelling: "Look at the fritters, hot and delicious, but the poor people can't afford them because the damned politicians are the ones with money which by the way, it's stolen money." What he said that day became famous throughout Sagua and people began repeating it.

95

On one occasion, "Cadera" went to Santa Clara, Las Villas's Province capital, and right in front of *La Caridad* Theatre, he began yelling" Finally, I'm in a town where no one calls me "Cadera, el loco."Everyone around there laughed a lot.

Another memorable character was "Sesé Sólis" who was half crazy. Her calves were very thin, so she wore socks full of straw to make them look normal. However, as she kept on walking, the straw kept going down all the way to her ankles and she looked ridiculously disgusting. People, then, would taunt her and say: "Sesé, only a tiger can make love to you," and she would reply: "And to your mother too."

MARÍA ELBA GONZÁLEZ: There were all kinds of characters in Remedios. Among them, there were three that stood out: "Pantera" ("Panther"), "Mariano matacucarachas" ("Mariano the Roach Killer") and "Masca Piedra" ("Rock Chewer"). "Pantera" claimed he was tough, but he really wasn't at all. "Mariano matacucarachas" used to sell water around town and he walked as if killing roaches. "Masca Piedra" was the town's gravedigger. People would scare children at night by telling them that he ate children.

RODOLFO SOTOLONGO: There were some salient characters in Colón. There was a bearded black guy who walked shoeless. They called him "Pata de Pisón" ("Lead Foot") because his feet were so wide and he walked so slowly. They also called him "Weyler[62]" because his beard reminded them of General Weyler's beard. Weyler was a despicable assassin who inflicted so much harm on Cuba.There was another one called "Juanfume," who rang the church bells while drunk. Also, no one would be able to forget

---

[62] Valeriano Weyler y Nicolau (1838-1930). Spanish Captain-General of Cuba from 1896 until 1897. In an effort to suppress Cuba's War of Independence, he implanted "The Reconcentration Policy" forcing Cuban peasant families to live in concentration camps in the city. Born in Palma de Mallorca, Spain, on September 17, 1838, he died in Madrid, on October 20, 1930.

"Cornelia Bofe" ("Cornelia the Unbearable"). She was a black drunk who was very nasty.

I think the most memorable was the one nicknamed "Siete Provincias" ("Seven Provinces"). I know how he got his nickname. This character, when he was young, asked a young lady to dance with him. Cuban young ladies during my time, wouldn't dance with individuals they didn't know. The young lady refused to dance with him, and he got upset. After a couple of seconds, he said to her:"Young lady, I must tell you that I have danced with young ladies like you, in Cuba's seven provinces." At that time, Cuba had only six provinces[63], so he showed his ignorance and from then on, they called him "Siete Provincias."

MARIO VEGA: I think the most famous folk character in Havana was "El Caballero de París."[64] ("The Paris Gentleman"). He was very famous. I saw him on Prado Boulevard many times and even spoke to him. Sure, he was mentally ill, but he could carry on an interesting conversation and could even recite poetry.

Another guy was "El Cojo del Capitolio" ("The Capitol Cripple"). This guy would ask for money right behind Cuba's capitol. If people didn't give him money, he would get out his megaphone and insult them. Additionally, he would hurl insults at politicians coming out of the capitol.

MARÍA ELBA GONZÁLEZ: In Santa Clara, there was the ever popular "El Burro Perico" ("Perico the Donkey"). His owner was a nice guy who let kids ride his donkey. As a matter of fact, all of the city's important people rode the donkey when they were kids. One day, an apple vendor parked his cart next to where "Perico" was

---

[63] Under the current regime, Cuba has been divided into 15 provinces.

[64] "El Caballero de París." (1899-1985). His real name was José María López Lledín. Born in Villaseca, Galicia, Spain, on December 30, 1899, he arrived in Cuba in 1913. This mentally deranged street wanderer is one of the most famous folk characters in Cuban history. It is still debatable how he acquired his name.

tied to the post and went in the store. When he came out, the donkey had eaten many apples. The man went crazy, started yelling and threatening to kill "Perico." However, a well-dressed man came by and said: "I'll pay you for all the apples the donkey has eaten, and I'll give you some extra money." He paid for them and it was all over.

Everyone loved that donkey. "Perico" would go to the main bars in town to drink beer. He would come to the bar, place his head on the counter and the bartender would serve him a bowl full of beer. One day the Polar Brewing Company, announced that all of the beer "Perico" consumed was going to be on the house. So, "Perico" became an important marketing tool for the brewery.The day "Perico" died was a very sad day in Santa Clara. Everyone went to his funeral. Even Fileno de Cárdenas, a congressman from Las Villas Province, came all the way from Havana to deliver the eulogy for the beloved "Perico."[65]

---

[65] Elio Fileno de Cárdenas Acosta was not a congressman, but rather a senator from Las Villas Province from 1940 until 1948.

MY FIRST JOB

CELESTINO SUÁREZ: When I finished grammar school, I began working at Ángel Calvo's hardware store. We opened at seven in the morning but I had to be up by five. I slept at the store and since I was the youngest one, they called me "El Cañonero" ("The Gunboat"). They called me that name, because like a gunboat, I had to be everywhere, doing everything.

In the morning, I had to go to the café around the corner and bring coffee for the other five employees in the store. Around nine in the morning, it was customary to drink *nicotel* and I was the one who made it. I would take six egg yolks, a liter of rum, a liter of water and a bit of sugar. Since I was the one who made it, I was the first one to taste it. So, from there on, I became used to *nicotel* and later in life, even today, I drink two to four ounces of rum in the morning and I'm fine.

It that store, I slept in a room surrounded by paint cans because the paint we sold was made there in that room. There was an employee who was nasty and mean, a real son-of-a-bitch. Once, I asked him to put the cans somewhere else because I was getting sick with that paint smell. However, he didn't do it or wouldn't even let me do it. As a result, I got sick, really sick.

One day, a man came and said: "I need a 4-inch heavy saw." I went to get the ladder and when I was on it, the mean guy yelled at me: "Hurry up, the gentleman has been waiting for half an hour." The customer hadn't even been waiting for a minute. I really got pissed off at the mean guy and from the top of the ladder I threw the whole box of saws at him. He ducked, and hit his head under the counter, but in doing so, he tipped an open red paint can. When he stuck his head out, it was all covered in red and the paint was dripping over his hair and the back of his head. I hadn't realized about the paint, so I thought the man was covered in blood. I came down from the ladder and started running all over the store, yelling out: "I killed him, I killed him!" Well, that was my last day working at the hardware store.

FÉLIX MEDINILLA: In Trinidad, I first started as a shoemaker apprentice. From there, I went on to become a clerk at a store owned by Nicanor Domínguez, Antonio Ruiz, Eduardo López and Enrique Rodríguez. Enrique Rodríguez was the one who taught me how to be a clerk. A poor man like me, without an education, never had a chance to make it in life. But my doctor, Dr. Carlos Oliva always told me: "Medinilla, you never had an education, but when you talk, people listen. Nature has endowed you with a superior intelligence. You are a self-taught man and a very wise man too."

FELIPE ROLOFF: One had to work very hard on our farm and my first job was driving an oxcart. One day, my father sold wood to a sugar mill and we only had oxcarts to deliver the wood. We loaded three or four oxcarts with big logs.

The trip usually took a day, but that time, because of the rain, it took us four days. It was something horrible because the carts got stuck in the mud. When a cart got stuck, one had to switch a team of oxen from another cart to pull it out of the mud. I would have to push from behind and others had to help me. An oxcart wheel is about eight feet tall and when one of those gets stuck in the mud, it takes a lot of work to free it. I wanted to leave the whole damned thing there, but I couldn't since the wood was our livelihood.

It took us four days to get there and the only thing we ate was mortadella with pieces of old bread. When we finally delivered the wood to the sugar mill, they treated us to rice and mortadella. There was no one in our group that could eat; we were so "fed up" with mortadella.

CEFERINO GARCÍA: I turned 18 in Sagua la Grande. My first job was that of sweeping the store floor. My other task was wrapping the products we sold. It was a hassle for me. One would think that wrapping things is easy, but it's not, especially if you don't know how to do it. From there, I worked behind the counter and also delivering groceries to our customers.

At first, I delivered groceries on foot and later when I learned to ride a bicycle I had to go all the way to the San Juan District with a basket full of groceries on top of the handlebars. It wasn't an easy task but it was much easier than delivering charcoal in a hand pushcart. I had to push that cart full of sacks all by myself. However, I didn't mind hard work and I loved the work because all I wanted was to learn. Thanks God, I've been able to improve myself throughout my life.

CARLOS MONTERO: My first job was in the military because I entered the Cuban Army Academy in 1912. Life in the academy was hard because our instructors were very demanding and Lezama[66], the academy's founder was very intelligent and strict.

Lezama wanted to turn a ragtag army into a professional one. He was one of the Cuban Army's great aces. We had to get up very early in the morning because Lezama was a no-nonsense guy. I'm always up at five in the morning because of Lezama. I graduated as Second Company Lieutenant in the Infantry Batallion.

ENRIQUE CASERO: One time I told my father: "Dad, I need to find a job. If you don't find me a job, then, I'll find one." Well, he found me a job at the Banco Español. My job consisted of collecting remissions from clients that they sent to the relatives in Spain and they sent them through the bank. At that time I was 15 years old and still wearing shorts.

I would walk the streets with wads full of money. One day, a man asked my father: "How in the hell do you allow your kid to go out on the streets with so much money? Don't you know he could get robbed?" My father calmly replied: "If anything hap-

---

[66] Eugenio Lezama. Father of the famous Cuban writer José Lezama Lima (1910-1976). He was a colonel and director of the Cuban Army Academy. He died in Pensacola, victim of the worldwide Spanish flu epidemic in 1919.

pens, I'll repay the money." At the time, there was no problem because he was well off.

There was a real problem and it was with the bank not paying me. It hadn't paid me in a month. Seeing that, I said to myself: "I'm not going back to work." One day, when my father returned from the farm he noticed something wrong with me and asked: "What's the matter with you?" I told him: "Dad, they haven't paid me yet. I'm not going back to work."

I didn't return to work and the bank officers asked my father: "Why isn't your son coming to work?" My father simply told them: "Because you haven't paid him." Then, they paid me. It was 30 *pesos* and my mother saved them for me to buy a "Palm Beach" brand suit to come over to the United States to study here, in this country.

MARÍA ELBA GONZÁLEZ: I received my law degree at a time when there were hardly any women lawyers in Cuba. The majority of those women lawyers worked for the government, but I was never one of them because I had my own practice. Criminal law gave you notoriety, but civil law gave you money. A civil lawyer, for example, did wills, trusts, and other things that brought money.

I remember that when I was beginning my career, the Clerk of Court, would give us cases involving petty theft and pickpocketing. One time, I had to defend a fellow accused of thievery who was quite a character. He knew the law much better than any of us lawyers. He would tell me: "Look, Madam, for the crime I've been charged, the maximum they can give me is 15 years in jail. I really haven't done a thing, so please, do a good job." I prepared the case quite well and he was acquitted. Afterwards, he came to me and said: "I don't have any money to pay you, but the first purse full of money that I'll steal, I'll give it to you."

MEALS, SWEETS, AND BEVERAGES

CEFERINO GARCÍA: I didn't know what going out for dinner meant because I ate breakfast, lunch and dinner at our general store. Over there, we cooked all kinds of beans and stews. There were two days where we ate the same meal. On Thursdays, we ate Galician style codfish and on Sundays it was Basque style codfish.

Our store used to lend money to small sugarcane growers. They would come up from faraway places to pay us and to buy goods from us and we served them lunch as a courtesy. We had a table that could fit 15 or 16 people. We would place a pitcher of wine at the end of the table and when each one was finished we served another one. We imported wine barrels from the Antonio Barceló winery in Spain.

CONCEPCIÓN VIGO: We sat at the table for breakfast, lunch, and dinner. We each had a designated seat at the table and we had to eat everything served at the table that my mother fed us. Besides our meals, my mother would give us an egg yolk with a small glass of vino Sansón[67] every day. She also made us drink German malt with condensed milk. She overfed us, but that's the way we were raised and I'm thankful for it.

FELIPE ROLOFF: We ate a lot of beef because we had a farm. We raised cattle, pigs, lambs and chicken and grew rice, beans, and all kinds of vegetables. We also made *tasajo* (jerked beef). We would slaughter a steer, slice the beef and salt it. The beef strips were then placed in a huge receptacle to cure for one or two weeks and then taken out to hang to dry in the sun.

---

[67] Spanish wine frequently given to 20th century Cuban children for its alleged restorative qualities.

During my times, people ate a lot of *tasajo* because it could be cooked in different ways. Some would cook it "pata de grillo" style (cricket legs style). The way this was made was to deep fry it in lard and with onions, garlic and other condiments. Another way of fixing it, was to serve it sort of like stew with tomato sauce, onions and peppers. That's the way it was served in the restaurants.

ANA AURORA RECIO: Our diet at home consisted mostly of beef. We ate roast beef, shredded beef with tomato sauce, fried shredded flank steak with onions and garlic and fried chickpeas. I've been to Spain three times and I've noticed they eat those types of food there. One thing, though, we never had beans at our home. We never cooked beans.

CELESTINO SUÁREZ: There was no lack of beef at our home because my father was a butcher. There were nine in our family and we would always eat eye of round beef roast stuffed with chorizo sausage. It was served with ripe fried plantains. We also ate Spanish omelets, chickpeas with rice, and codfish. The thing we really loved were the sweet pastries. My mother especially loved them. The first question she would ask my father when he returned from work was: "Manuel, did you bring me any sweet pastries?"

RODOLFO SOTOLONGO: On our farm, we ate all kinds of Cuban food. We would slaughter a steer and make *tasajo* out of it. We put the beef strips inside huge clay bins filled with lard so that it wouldn't spoil prior to being cured in the fresh air. We had no refrigeration so that was the only way to do it.

MANUEL GARCÍA IGLESIAS: My mother made all kinds of sweets. She didn't bake them, she used a terra-cotta dish. To make *cascos de guayaba* (guava shells), she used fresh guavas and *boniatillo*, made with a type of boiled sweet potato, sugar and cinnamon which was delicious. Her *dulce de leche* was simply exquisite. She would take curdled sour milk, add sugar and cinnamon to it and slowly heat all that stuff. It was delicious!

VÍCTOR VEGA CEBALLOS: *Arroz Camagüeyano* (Camagüeyan style rice) is something special. This dish is made with rice and chicken, although some make it with beef. Chicken broth is added to the rice and as it's being cooked, olives, raisins, and almonds are added. The key to this dish lives in cooking the rice so that the grain is neither hard nor sticky. It's delicious!

We also ate roasted pork which was Camagüey's typical dish. Unlike other Cubans, Camagüeyans didn't add *mojo* (garlic and oil sauce). The pig was roasted and nothing was added to it and when it was ready to be served, salt would be added.

The way the pig was roasted was for a hole to be dug in the ground and it was filled with charcoal. Two vertical poles would be at the end and the entire dressed pig placed in a horizontal spit between the two poles. The pig would be turned slowly over and over. It was a very slow roasting process and the fire couldn't be set too high, so as not to burn the meat. By roasting it slowly, the grease would drip drop by drop and the meat would be juicy and not greasy at all.

In Camagüey, we had another dish called *pastelón*. It was sort of like a type of chicken pot pie. Making it was a time-consuming labor. The person making it would have to knead the dough slowly, calculate when it was ready and then, add chicken or beef along with many condiments and bake it. It was great!

In Camagüey, there was something called *mazamorra*. It was made with cornmeal, sugar, grated cheese and a bit of butter. Once it was ready it was cut into chunks and served. It was both delicious and nutritious because with *mazamorra* chunk and a glass of milk, one could last the whole day.

In Camagüey, when I was young, our daily bread was *casabe,* made out of yucca. I ate it with homemade butter. I first ate commercially made butter when I went to study in Havana. Camagüey was cattle country, so there was plenty of milk there. Since there was no refrigeration, milk had to be boiled twice a day, once in the morning, and once in the afternoon. When milk is boiled, it has thick butterfat in. I would take that skin and eat it with peaches or *mamey* (mamme apple), be it red or yellow on the inside. Sometimes, I would eat it plain with just a little bit of sugar. I had a friend who was grossed out by just the side of that butterfat skin. So for her, milk had to be sieved three times. It was done in a cloth sieve. I was raised eating all of these things. The majority of Camagüeyans were raised like me. Some of them are proud of that, but there are some who wouldn't admit it.

MARIO VEGA: During Machado's dictatorship economic conditions were bad in Cuba, so we had nothing to eat but cornmeal. It was cornmeal for breakfast, lunch, and dinner. Cornmeal at dinner was served with *boniato* with a bit of sugar added to it. I became so fond of cornmeal that even when the good times returned I would eat cornmeal daily. Everyone had to eat cornmeal for six or seven months because Machado wouldn't pay civil service employees.

GRACIELA DUBROCQ: No dish is more authentically Cuban than *ajiaco*. It's a dish that practically has all of the vegetables grown in Cuba. To make a good *ajiaco*, a big pot with broth is fundamental. Right in that broth, pork chunks and *tasajo* are added. Later, after the broth is boiled, green plantains, *yucca*, corn and *malanga* (elephant ear root) are added. When these ingredients have softened out, more ingredients such as squash, potatoes, ripe plantains and sweet potatoes are added. Finally, a little bit of *bijol* (achiato powder) is added to give the *ajiaco* some coloring. In Cuba, there was a saying that went like this: "I placate my appetite with *ajiaco* that's done quite right."

ENRIQUE CASERO: In Cuba, there were many types of beverages that were homemade. For example there was *aguajola* which was a beverage made out of water, honey, cinnamon and sugar. In Oriente Province, there was another beverage called *Pru* It was brewed out of fermented plant roots. It was very tasty and medicinal.

    The Spaniards made a beverage called *bul* which was made out of beer, ginger and lime. There was also *chicha* which was made out of pineapple skin, sugar and spice. It was very refreshing and pretty tasty. Of course, we had all kinds of fruit milkshakes because *El Caney* is in Oriente Province and that area is where the world's best fruits are grown.

REMEDIES

HORTENSIA LÓPEZ: When a child had a bellyache, they would take two slices of bread mixed with powdered cinnamon and cooking wine. Then, they would place them on the child's belly. The toasts' warmth, together with the wine's soothing warmth, would make the child sleepy and soon, the colic would disappear.

Another household remedy were the *plantillas*. The *plantillas* were booties made out of cloth and they would put an ointment made out of mutton tallow inside them. The booties would cover the child's feet and they, in turn would be covered with socks. *Plantillas* were used to get rid of a high fever. Once the *plantillas* were used on a child, there was no more fever the next day. People also used star anise for stomach ache and linden leaves to calm down nerves.

I have a very interesting real story that happened to me. My stepson –may he rest in peace– was once gravely ill. I mean gravely ill. He contracted pneumonia when he went to the Santiago Nautical Club. When he returned, our neighbor noticed he had a cold, but he told her: "It's nothing, I'll take a bath and I'll be fine." However, late in the evening, he got really sick, very sick. A group of doctors was brought in and while the doctors were consulting among themselves, he told them that he couldn't urinate.

The next day, a lady came by home and said: "If you want the boy to urinate you have to prepare an infusion made out of cricket's legs." I was so desperate that I didn't know what to do. So, I made that concoction which was like a strained warm drink, and he drank it. In the evening, he urinated, and from then on, he got better. When he finally got over his pneumonia, he was pale, and his side was tilted, but the cricket's legs infusion saved him.

MARÍA ELBA GONZÁLEZ: I'm going to tell a story about a household remedy. One day, while peeling a sugarcane stalk, I cut myself badly with a knife. Our servant came out running with cobweb in her hands. She wrapped my finger around it, and it stopped the bleeding. I didn't have to have stitches. The cobweb did it!

In my home, we cured everything with household remedies. Very rarely the doctor visited the home. There was something we did to cure an *empacho* (indigestion). It consisted of laying the individual down on his stomach, then someone would pull the skin from his or her back sides and once the skin made a popping sound, the *empacho* was cured.

There were lots of remedies to cure a cold. One of them was very easy to make. One would make a concoction using sour orange leaves. Another was similar, but using eucalyptus leaves. Once either remedy was taken, the cold and the fever were gone.

If a person had a muscle ache, it was customary to use a kind of plaster with mutton tallow ointment and put it right where it hurt. If a person had a very high fever, they would put over his or her head a dry biscuit sprinkled with cooking wine. This was done to prevent a brain hemorrhage caused by the fever. I saw that with my own eyes when my sister contracted typhoid fever.

RODOLFO SOTOLONGO: In Cuba, there was a plant called *mastuerzo* (cress) which was good for the kidneys. Another good one was corn husk because it was a good diuretic. Sea grape was also used to treat diarrhea.

There was also a plant called *sábila* (aloe) which had anti-inflammatory properties. Scientists today have proven that this is true. Now, there are two types of aloe. One is originally from the Cape of Good Hope and the other one is originally from Barbados. The Barbadian one was used a lot in Cuba to treat burns and skin lesions. It was also used as a laxative. The aloe's jelly is very bitter, and they would put it on children's fingers so that they would be unable to suck them.

RICARDO COBIÁN: I am a pharmacist and we used to prepare all kinds of remedies at the pharmacy. At that time, there were hardly any pills so that remedies were based on plants medicinal properties. For example, we would prepare *tintura de belladonna* (Belladona Tincture) which is a herbaceous plant used as in analgesic to treat stomach cramps. In order to treat diarrhea, we would make Gouger powder which contained opium.

Pharmaceutical products used in Cuba were mostly made in France. In fact, the most commonly used cough syrup was Ticol; it was a cough syrup made by Roche, a French pharmaceutical company. It's no longer in use.

I don't know about all these kinds of drugs and medicines we use nowadays. One sees animals in the wilderness and they live fine, without vaccines or antibiotics. So, if you are out in the wilderness, there are no illnesses, but if you are out in the middle of civilization, that's when you have all kinds of illnesses.

During my times, people depended more on the pharmacist than on the doctor. In Minas, Pinar del Río Province, there were no doctors and I had to play the role of doctor. People would travel miles and miles by either boat or horseback to come and see me many times, and I usually would not even charge them a penny.

Ricardo Cobián, c. 1950s
(Courtesy of Dr. Alberto Hernández Chiroldes)

STORES

HORTENSIA LÓPEZ: My father had a general store in El Caney, but he never let us go out there because all kinds of people went there, good and not so good. I would not go in the store, but I could always see men sitting in *taburetes* outside the store singing *décimas*. One of them would sing a *décima*[68] while playing a guitar and as soon as he was finished, the other would reply with a different *décima*. It was sort of like a contest and would go on forever.

At the general store it was customary to give regular customers the *ñapa* (a treat) when they purchased something. It was a way for the owner to thank clients. The majority of the clients asked for *raspadura* (a sweet made out of brown sugar).

MANUEL GARCÍA IGLESIAS: My grandfather had a general store which was mostly a toy store. It was named "El amigo de niños." ("The Kids' Friend"). At that time, my grandfather was a celebrity among kids. They would flock to his store and he would give them a piece of candy as the *ñapa*. Indeed, that justified his store's name.

VÍCTOR VEGA CEBALLOS: Store clerks were merely the owner's slaves. Generally, they were treated unfairly and had to work many hours. However, things began to change when Cuba became a republic. A Camagüeyan legislator named Arteaga[69] was credited with the eight- hour workday. Yet, there were stores in Camagüey that secretly opened until 11 in the evening.

---

[68] A ten-line stanza impromptu poem traditionally sung by Cuban peasants.

[69] Emilio Arteaga Quesada (1873-?) Member of the Cuban House of Representatives from Camagüey Province during the early years of the Cuban Republic. He was known for his progressive legislative measures.

Antonio Inclán had a grocery store around the corner. I remember going there to shop for something after closing hours. I had to be very careful because if the police were to find out that the store was open after closing hours, they would fine him.

There were two types of stores: the grocery store and the general store. The products sold at the grocery store were mostly food products so what it sold was more limited. On the other hand, at the general store, one could find almost anything ranging from a piece of fatback to an embroidered dress.

Grocery stores and general stores had zinc counters. On the countertop, there were clay pitchers, so that clients could have a drink of water if they were thirsty. The pitchers were chained to prevent them from being stolen. Important gentlemen from town would go to their favorite grocery or general store to have a *draque* which was a shot of gin with soda water. It was usual to see one of these gentlemen dressed with his alpaca coat, his pair of white pants, his straw hat and his *cocomacaco*[70] having his *draque* at the store in the morning

MARIO VEGA: Liquor was served at both the grocery store and the general store. One would go to either store and ask the owner or a clerk: "Please, serve the guy over there a shot of rum." One didn't even know the guy, but it was a way of meeting people. I used to go to the clerk and tell him: "How about a beer for this guy –give him a bottle of beer and it's on me." That's the sense of hospitality we had in Cuba. That sense of friendship and brotherhood has been lost here.

CEFERINO GARCÍA: Our general store opened at six in the morning and closed at eight in the evening. At times, there were regular customers who were returning from the theater and had forgotten to buy something during the day and wanted to get it af-

---

[70] A twisted knotty wooden cane used by well-to-do Cubans and politicians during the early years of the Cuban Republic.

ter we closed. Since it was usual for us to sit and chat in front of the store after closing hours, one of us would get up, and get what he wanted from the store. There was no other way; one had to do it because they were our regular customers.

Right in front of the store we had posts to tie the customers' horses. It was there, in the store, where I learned to carry huge slabs of *tasajo* and put them in the packsaddles. We used to sell large quantities of *tasajo* because it was the peasants' traditional staple food. *Tasajo*, rice and *boniato* were always present at a peasant's table.

**Ceferino García with nephews, c. 1930s
(Courtesy of Manuel García Ávila)**

COMETS, HURRICANES, FIRES, AND CALAMITIES

HORTENSIA LÓPEZ: Halley's Comet[71] was one of the most beautiful things I've ever seen in my life. When people began talking about Halley's Comet, Cuban newspapers were always late reporting it. The information we received about this phenomenon came from the Spanish magazine "Blanco y Negro." That magazine would give one detailed information.

As the comet's day was approaching, we would place mattresses on our terrace and lay on our backs trying to see it. Finally, the comet appeared one evening and it was beautiful. Its tail was big, similar to a horse's tail. It had a green light which we had never seen.

In Santiago, they just had installed electric light which was yellowish in color. So, seeing the comet with that green light was awesome. It appeared very fast and left very fast. It started to descend behind the "Los Angeles Clinic" and Saint Ann's Church and then it disappeared. People were afraid and they were saying that it was going to be the end of the world, but nothing happened. I hope to see it again.

RICARDO COBIÁN: I saw Haley's Comet. It coincided with the Rural Guard garrison's explosion in Pinar del Río. Many people got killed and people said the comet had caused the explosion, but it was an accident.

---

[71] Discovered by British astronomer Edmund Halley (1658- 1742), the comet is characterized by the reappearance every 75 years. The last time it reappeared was in 1986

The Abuelos

HORTENSIA LÓPEZ: Once there was a tremor in the Santiago area. It was not an earthquake, just a tremor, but people became very scared and went out on the streets. I think it happened on Maundy Thursday, but buildings shook three or four times. My youngest sister had given birth to a baby girl, and as the baby was being breast-fed, the tremors caused her to choke and for a few days, she couldn't breathe right. We took her all the way to Havana to save her life.

JOSEFINA PÉREZ: Once, next to our home, a huge fire broke out. There was a man whose last name was Reitor. He had a confectionery store next to our home. I went there in the morning to get change for a centén[72] and told him: "Don Pepe, the glass case is all empty." He told me: " It's been the best day of the year, we are completely sold out."

Around midnight we heard someone yelling: "Help! Help!" It was Don Pepe. His store was on fire and threatening to spread to our home. We got out and started yelling: "Fire! Fire!" The ice factory on Dorticós's Street, right on the corner of Prado Street, sounded the alarm and firefighters came in their horse wagon trying to put out the fire.

There was an old man named Pedro Corpión; he was our neighbor on the other side. He had a lot of money, and he started arguing with the firefighters because he wanted them to spray his home with water so it wouldn't catch on fire. The fire chief got very angry at him and told him: "Look, sir, you are rich, you have lots of properties, you have everything; but this family has nothing but this house, so we will have to save their house first." The firefighters were very nice and saved our home.

---

[72] Spanish colonial coin, equivalent to 10 reales. The centén continued to be used during the early days of the Cuban Republic and was equivalent to five pesos.

VÍCTOR VEGA CEBALLOS: I remember a sad happening in Camagüey and that was the Spanish flu[73]. That epidemic hit Camagüey very hard at the end of 1918 and the beginning of 1919. They called it the Spanish flu, but it had nothing to do with Spain. It actually started a bit before the end of World War I in the European battlefields.

A ship had come from Hamburg to the Camagüeyan port of Nuevitas. That ship had some sailors on board who had been infected with the flu. In fact, some of them had died on their way to Cuba. At that time, there was no such thing as a quarantine, much less in Nuevitas.

As the flu began to spread throughout Camagüey, it gave way to a popular tune around the area which went like this:

> A ship from Hispana Grey[74]
> Has arrived in Camagüey
> It's bringing this evil thing
> And the alarm has to ring
> So singers let's begin to sing
> And cognac we have to drink.

The tune was a product of the popular belief that drunks weren't susceptible to that illness. Other people thought that both rum and cognac were preventers of such an illness. As a result, liquor sales in Camagüey skyrocketed. Additionally, people began carrying a small alum stone in their pockets, for it was said that it protected them from the Spanish flu. I remember that home floors were swept and mopped with creolin. In the morning, kids were given Gavarcine Ducat pills which was a French remedy against colds.

---

[73] The Spanish influenza of 1918, is a misnomer, since it did not start in Spain. It's alleged to have been brought to Europe by an American captain at the end of World War I. Because the Spanish Royal family contracted the illness, it was named Spanish flu. Over 50 million people died worldwide as a result of the illness.

[74] Cuban mispronunciation of Grace. The Grace Shipping Line was one of the most important lines in the first half of the 20th century.

Panic spread throughout Camagüey. Theaters closed their doors and even churches closed down. I remember walking around town and it was scary because there were black ribbons on the doors of homes where someone had died. The city also ran out of wood because of the number of coffins that had to be made and even wooden wardrobes became invaluable commodities because the wood was used to make coffins.

During the ordeal, there was a man whose body burst at his home because there was no coffin to bury him. The family left the home and left the poor dead man to rot there. Moreover, there was a woman who lived outside the city. Her husband had died from the Spanish flu and her children also had the illness. She went crazy, took a machete and killed them. She also tried to commit suicide, but the police got there and arrested her. They put her in jail but she died of her self-inflicted wounds later.

MANUEL GARCÍA IGLESIAS: The 1933 hurricane is still on my mind. I had arrived in Sagua that day because I had been named Secretary of the Electoral Board. While I was at City Hall, a telegram from Cuba's National Observatory arrived. It stated that there was a hurricane moving towards the Cuban northern coast and warned that people needed to take proper measures. However, people paid little attention.

More telegrams kept coming warning people. In the late afternoon, I was visiting a friend and the firefighters' truck came around with the siren blaring. I immediately went to my cousin's home to face the hurricane there. We started to protect the home and barred the front door. The next morning I saw sparks near the home, but I didn't know what was going on. A minute later, as I looked up, I realized that the Morón coffee roasting business was on fire.

The hurricane came in between the evening of August 31 and September 1 at dawn. One must recognize the tremendous help provided by the United British Railroads to the port of Isabela de Sagua. The port was right in the middle of the hurricane's path, so the railroad officials ordered several trains to evacuate the people from Isabela. As a matter of fact, the people who were on the last train had to weather the hurricane at the Sagua train station because the wind began to rock the train cars just as they were approaching the station. That railroad company saved those people because Isabela was practically destroyed by the hurricane.

The situation was even worse in Cayo Cristo, a key not far from Isabela. There were more than 30 people spending the last days of the summer season in that resort key and nearly all of them died because they ignored the warnings. At Cayo Cristo, there was Dr. Arroyo who had been spending the summer there. That morning he had heard the observatory warnings and went around the key yelling out: "I've heard the hurricane warnings, let's get out, people you've got to get out!" Well, the people didn't listen to him; instead, they listened to José Bory a veteran vacationer who told them there was nothing to worry about. He even said: "Look, it's a beautiful day out here today." Indeed, it was a beautiful day and since Bory, who owned a pharmacy on Martí Street, right on the corner of Solís Street, was well respected, people decided to stay.

During the late afternoon, things began to change. Waves began pounding the shore and no boat captain dared to come to Cayo Cristo to evacuate those who had decided to remain. As the hours passed, the storm surge, together with the wind began to take a toll on the summer homes. In the evening, things turned for the worse and as the survivors told me, the residents, as a last-ditch effort, formed a human chain to protect themselves, but the waves swept them away.

Miraculously, there were two survivors. There was Pascualito Pérez, the photographer Pascual Pérz's son and a young black who was their cook's son. As the wind increased, they held on to a mangrove for hours. Pascualito remembers that his friend would yell at him: "Hold on, Pascualito, hold on!" It was a miracle how they saved their lives because over 35 people died there. The whole key was split in two. After that tragedy, no one spent their summers in Cayo Cristo. They would go to nearby Cayo Esquivel at the time. Nature is something else - something else.

An interesting event happened as a result of that hurricane. Cuban Interim President, Dr. Carlos Manuel de Céspedes[75] went to Sagua to assess this situation and help the victims. In fact, I was in the delegation that went to greet the president and take him to the Hotel Sagua. While he was talking with us, a group of teachers heard he was in town, and they came to see him demanding a salary increase. That was rather laughable; there was the president, assessing hurricane damages and then came the teachers demanding a salary increase.

That day, a banquet was going to be held in his honor, but there was hardly any food at the hotel and the manager had very little cash on hand to buy food. Interim Mayor Castellanos pledged that the city was going to pay for the costs, so the people went out to get chickens because they were going to serve arroz con pollo (chicken and rice). People went all over town looking for chickens because there were none in the market. So, they had to requisition them from people who had chicken coops at their homes. The banquet was held; but, unfortunately, for Céspedes, when he returned to Havana, Batista[76] had already staged his famous September 4, 1933 coup.

MARÍA ELBA GONZÁLEZ: The 1932 earthquake hit Santiago de Cuba very hard. Although there were buildings made out of

---

[75] Carlos Manuel de Céspedes y Quesada (1871-1939). Cuban Liberation Army Colonel and son of Carlos Manuel de Céspedes, "the Father of the Country." He was Interim President of Cuba from August 13, 1933 until his overthrow by Fulgencio Batista on September 4, 1933. Born in New York City, on August 12 1871, he died in Havana on March 28, 1939.

[76] Fulgencio Batista y Zaldívar (1901-1973). Cuban Army Sergeant who staged the September 4, 1933 coup. Known as the "Strong Man of Cuban Politics," Batista was the ultimate power broker of Cuban politics from 1933 until 1959. He was democratically elected president in 1940. However, in 1952, he staged another coup and ruled Cuba until January 1, 1959 when he was defeated by Fidel Castro. Born in Banes, Oriente Province, on January 16, 1901, he died in exile in Guadalmina, Spain, on August 6, 1973.

steel and concrete, they were destroyed. It just happened that my husband and I were visiting there and witnessed it.

We were at a hotel and the room began shaking and when it was over, we noticed that the only room that wasn't damaged was ours. I took our suitcases and told my husband: "Throw them out of the window into the street. I'm not staying here, I'm leaving." When we left, there were more aftershocks. It was the biggest earthquake up to that date in Cuba. There is talk about Santiago disappearing from the face of the earth if another earthquake hits.

MANUEL GARCÍA IGLESIAS: One of the most tragic events that I will always remember was the day that a group of young ladies dressed in chicken costumes burned to death at a dance. That happened in Sagua in 1929. I got to my home in Clara Barton Street around 10 in the evening. Suddenly, I noticed a lot of people running on Colón Street. They were screaming that some people had been burned to death at a dance.

The tragedy happened at "Edén Sport," a social club for blacks. A dance was being held there and a comparsa of young black ladies came in dressed in chicken costumes. Those costumes were made out of cotton and apparently there were people with sparklers around the dance floor. One of the costumes caught on fire which quickly spread to those wearing the costumes. Nine of them were burned to death.

I was a senior at Martí school, a private school, and we all went to the funeral. We all wore military uniforms. All of the social clubs in Sagua suspended their events and Cuban flags flew at half mast. Firetrucks carrying their coffins drove to the cemetery and many people accompanied the funeral procession on foot. It was a sad event, a total tragedy.

SUPERSTITIONS, RITES, AND CEREMONIES

RODOLFO SOTOLONGO: There were a number of superstitions in Cuba. They were not exclusively Cuban because I'm sure other countries have the same superstitions. There was one about Tuesday, the 13th. People would say: "On Tuesday, the 13^{th,} never get married, never travel and never be away from your family."Another superstition was that of not walking under a ladder. If there was a ladder on a sidewalk, a person stepped off of the sidewalk and walked around it. People said that to walk under a ladder would bring bad luck.

MANUEL GARCÍA IGLESIAS: In Cuba, there was a very interesting superstition and that was not letting a rocking chair rock by itself. If someone got up from a rocking chair and it kept rocking, someone else would come and stop it from rocking. It was said that a rocking chair, rocking by itself, would bring bad luck. For example, I, myself, would go out and immediately stop it.

There was another one dealing with water. Many people, on New Year's Eve, would go and throw out a bucketful of water into the street to get rid of evil spirits. I think those people added basil to the water because they believed that the basil was good for getting rid of evil spirits. I don't know what made them think that, but they kept on doing it.

CELESTINO SUÁREZ: Superstitions are perennial in every country and Cuba was no exception. Some say that superstitions came to Cuba via the African slaves, but there were many Spanish who were *ñañigos*[77]. I believe that superstitions are part of being human because human beings need to believe in those things.

---

[77] Members of the Abakuá Secret Society, an Afro-Cuban cult. The misappropriated word was also used to identify a person who practiced witchcraft.

In Cuba, many people believed in witchcraft and sorcery. For example, it was said that if someone put roasted toad powder or cemetery dirt in someone else's coffee cup, that person was going to be a mess for the rest of his life. Also, if a *mayombero* (sorcerer) took a dead child's spirit and put it inside a doll, it would harm people. They called that *chichericú*, but I don't believe in any of that.

ENRIQUE CASERO: Over in our farm, there was a fortune teller who would come every Thursday night and lots of people from neighboring farms would come over to see him. He would be over at the farmhands' barracks and it wasn't unusual to see 300 or 400 horses tied to posts and trees there. The place was always packed because he claimed to be a *curandero* (healer).

Many peasant young ladies would go to see him and ask him to prescribe herbal remedies for them or for him to intercede so that their wishes would be granted. Well, it was his wishes that were granted, because he got a lot of them pregnant.

I don't know how much of a fortune teller or healer he was, but as far as I'm concerned, he was a real son-of-a-bitch. He was illiterate, and one time, he asked me to write for him the remedies he prescribed such as basil, cloves, garlic and many herbs for this and that. I did it, but I don't believe in that crap.

FELIPE ROLOFF: In the countryside, there were all kinds of superstitions and the peasants believed in fortune tellers. These people did not charge for their services but the peasants would bring them chickens or some other gifts. There was an older woman called "Bernarda, la adivina" ("Bernarda, the Fortune Teller"). Peasants would come from afar to see her. I don't know why, but she was famous. As far as I know, she was both uneducated and incompetent. In other words, she was a farce.

MARÍA ELBA GONZÁLEZ: In Cuba, there was something called *el mal de ojo* (the evil eye). This was a spell caused by someone who wanted to do evil. That person would come to someone else's home and if he or she saw a plant, for example, she would look at it, pay a compliment, and within a short time, the plant would wither away. One time I witnessed this when a woman came to my home. We had this beautiful red pepper plant and she said: "What a beautiful little plant!" A while later, after she left, the plant was dead.

In order to neutralize the evil eye, an *azabache* (jet trinket) was used. We made kids wear an *azabache,* because kids were most vulnerable to the evil eye. When someone who possessed the evil eye would compliment a kid, and the *azabache,* suddenly, would break, it meant the evil eye was cast on the kid. However, by breaking, the *azabache* sacrificed itself to stop the evil eye.

I can assure you that an episode regarding the evil eye happened to me with my daughter. When she was about one, our messenger boy used to take her to the park in the stroller. One day, when they returned from the park, I noticed that her *azabache* was broken. I said to him: "Hey, I noticed that her *azabache* is broken." He then, said to me: "Well, there was a lady in the park who held her and was complimenting her." Suddenly I said: "Oh, my God! The *azabache* really protected her!" This is something that I believe in and nobody is going to take this away from me.

The people suffering from the evil eye would normally experience a high fever. So the prayer to San Luis Beltrán[78] had to be said. To say the prayer one had to find three ladies named María. They would be the ones saying the prayer. I don't know why, but that prayer cured many from the evil eye.

RODOLFO SOTOLONGO: Out in the countryside there was always a *bembé*[79]. In our farm there was a place called "Los Congos" because it was a former *batey*[80] where Congolese slaves used

---

[78] San Luis Beltrán (1526-1581). Dominican Friar who lived in South America during the 16th century. The prayer to him is used by many to ask for his intercession in curing maladies attributed to the evil eye.

[79] Feast or religious ceremony of African origin.

[80] Place around a farm or sugar mill where slaves first were housed and later where sugar mill field workers and farmhands dwelled.

to live during Spanish colonial times. Many of them had been my grandfather's slaves and their descendants who kept their *batey* there, had their *bembé's* there because my father would give them his permission. I remember the constant drumbeat. My brothers and I would go there galloping on our horses to see a *bembé*. Over there, they had *Santería* ceremonies. Those ceremonies were open to the public but it was forbidden to enter where the *santero* (*Santería priest*) was going to be initiated as a priest.

MANUEL GARCÍA IGLESIAS: I went to a *bembé* a few times. In Sagua, over the Backer Boulevard, towards the right, there was a place called "Corrolungo." There were a lot of blacks in that place and they would have their dances, accompanied by drumbeat. They would drink heavily and dance whirling all around until one of them would fall. When one of them had fallen, it was said that he or she had been possessed by an African deity. However, the real truth was that the individual had fallen from exhaustion.

CUBAN LEGENDS

FELIX MEDINILLA: Trinidad is known for the Holy Week processions. On Maundy Thursday, there was the "Cristo de la Veracruz" ("Christ of the True Cross") procession. The crucified Christ's statue would be brought out of the church and the procession would follow it around town.

There is something interesting about that statute which depicts the crucified Christ. During Spanish colonial times, that statute was to be shipped to Veracruz, Mexico, but the statute didn't want to go. Every time a ship would come to take it away, there would be a terrible storm full of wind, thunder and lightning. As a result, the ship would have to stay in port. The fact was that Christ wanted to stay in Trinidad. Finally, authorities gave up and the statue stayed in Trinidad. I wasn't even born during that time. I really want to go there again so I can kiss it.

FELIPE ROLOFF: In Camagüey, there was Father Valencia, a Spanish priest. This man who lived during Spanish colonial times was always helping the poor, especially the elderly. In the late afternoon, after he finished collecting money for the poor and for the home he built for the elderly, he would go to feed his pigeons because he loved birds.

One day, Father Valencia died, but every afternoon, as if were time to feed the birds, a white vulture would appear, circling the city. According to many, the white vulture represented Father Valencia's soul watching over the poor and the elderly.

MARÍA ELBA GONZÁLEZ: In Santa Clara, there was a cane maker who would whiten the cane with limestone. One day, he tried to whiten a wooden cane, but no matter how hard he tried, he couldn't do it. The next day, he looked at the cane, and to his astonishment there was Christ's image on it. Carefully, he cut the image out of the cane and built a glass shrine for it. People in Santa Clara began calling it "El Santo del Palo" ("The Wooden Cane Saint") and began worshiping it.

It was said that praying to it, miracles would happen. Arquímedes Pous[81], for example, had lost his voice and after praying to the image, he recovered his voice. As a token of gratitude, he offered his precious emerald collection to the shrine. The home was full of relics from the devout followers. I remember seeing it; the image had so many relics.

However, one night, a thief entered the home and put a number of relics in his sack. He escaped, but when he reached the street corner, he tripped and hit his head against the curb and died instantly. He left behind a sack full of relics and jewelry.

There was another legend called "La Virgen del Coco" ("Our Lady of Coconut"). There was a fallen coconut at a place called "Los Pilongos" and someone there cracked a coconut and opened it. Inside that coconut, in its white flesh, there was the image of *La Virgen de la Caridad*. People took pictures of it and that story is in the Santa Clara local history books.

CONCEPCIÓN VIGO: Guantánamo also has its legend. There are some very good rivers there. In the Guaso River there is a fish called *jotú*. When someone who is not from Guantánamo comes to the city and drinks water from the Guaso and eats the fish, that person stays in Guantánamo.

RODOLFO SOTOLONGO: Between Boca de Camarioca and the La Maya Lighthouse near Matanzas, there is a shallow rocky inlet known for its rough waters. If a boat gets wrecked up there, it will be torn to pieces. During Spanish colonial times, in that inlet, slaves were smuggled.

---

[81] Arquímedes Pous (1891-1926). One of the great figures of Cuban Vaudeville. Born in Cienfuegos, Las Villas Province, on May 18, 1891, he died in Mayagüez, Puerto Rico, on April 16, 1926.

There was an elderly British man named Johnny who lived around there, right on the Casañas family farm. He had come to the area in one of those smuggling operations. Johnny was nearly 100 years old and used to tell me that they called the place "the Graveyard" because of the many people who had drowned there. Johnny would also tell me that at night, one could hear the slaves' chains and shackles rattling. And when there was a full moon, the slaves' ghosts would appear.

CELESTINO SUÁREZ: In Cienfuegos there was a very popular legend known as "La Dama Azul del Castillo de Jagua" ("The Lady in Blue from the Jagua Castle Fortress"). There are numerous versions of it, and I don't know if mine is the right one, but I'll tell it anyway.

When the fortress was being built, every night, in the moonlight, an elegant lady's ghost dressed in blue would appear around the fortress's terrace. There were soldiers there but, obviously, no one wanted to be on sentry duty. One day a cocky Spanish lieutenant scolded the soldiers; calling them a bunch of cowards and telling them that he was going to show them how to be a man. So, he went to the top of the fortress on guard duty. At around midnight, the "Lady in Blue" appeared. The next morning, they found the cocky lieutenant lying on his side, completely unconscious. But, that wasn't all, next to him was a skeleton wearing a blue dress. People say that every night when there is a full moon, the "Lady in Blue" ghost strolls around the fortress.

MANUEL GARCÍA IGLESIAS: Sagua was very famous for the "El Guije" legend. Towards the right riverbank there were rocks forming treacherous rapids and that's where "El Guije" supposedly lived, although no one ever saw this creature. Everyone imagined "El Guije" to be a grotesque toadlike creature with huge paws and fangs. Supposedly, every Good Friday he would come out and if he saw someone bathing in "the Guije's" pond —as it's dwelling place was called— he would grab the person and with his paws he would drown the victim.

People were terrified of that place and wouldn't go there because they were afraid of the "Guije." All in all, it wasn't true. It's true that many years ago, someone drowned in that place. I remember reading that apparently in Africa a similar legend existed and it was transplanted to Cuba by the African slave population that lived around the river.

There were also the Sagua ghosts. When I was a boy they said that there were a lot of ghosts in Sagua. They said that there was a ghost around Backer Boulevard and another one in the Coco Solo District. However, I had a friend who had been a policeman in Sagua; and he told me that there were ghosts dressed in white. Well, he said that they weren't really ghosts, but rather men who were having extramarital affairs with certain ladies.

These men would dress in white sheets to scare people away so they would get lost. Since nobody would be watching where they were going, they wouldn't get caught "consummating" their extramarital affairs.

Manuel García, fourth from left, 1978
(Courtesy of *El Undoso*)

VÍCTOR VEGA CEBALLOS: I have a very interesting legend. It's called "The Home Where the Crime was Committed." I know it very well because that home was right across the street from our home. In fact, the people who dwelled there were relatives.

The man who lived there was very rich and handsome, but was very prejudiced. He fell in love with the daughter of a well-to-do family. However, her family didn't want her to marry him because he was very biased. He, for instance, used to say that black slaves didn't have a soul because they weren't humans. People would argue with him by saying that slaves were humans because they could talk, but, he would always reply: "Parrots also can talk by imitating sounds."

All of this was happening when the abolition of slavery issue was on the Cuban political agenda. The young lady's family who were abolitionists didn't want their beautiful, well-educated and fine daughter to marry such an idiot even if he were more handsome than Adonis[82] or richer than Cressus[83]. However, the young lady married him.

After their marriage, they had two sons and a daughter. In her next pregnancy, she gave birth to twin boys. However, the couple was having marriage problems because he was very cruel and mistreated the slaves. Those slaves had been property of his wife's family and had been given to him as a dowry. Seeing how badly he was behaving, she warned him by saying: "If you mistreat Encarnación and Tomasa, that will be the end of our marriage because I will not allow you to enter my bedroom anymore."

Diego, as he was named, never heeded the warning and he just laughed at it. Not only did he mistreat the two slave women, but forced them to have sex with him in order to have mulatto children. In those days of slavery, mulattoes brought a higher amount of money for the master because they were sold for higher prices than blacks.

---

[82] Character in Greek mythology famous for his handsomeness.

[83] King of Lydia, famous for his wealth.

When the twins were born, the couple got two black female slaves who had recently given birth as wet nurses. At that time, it was believed that if babies were breast-fed by black female slaves, they would be stronger and healthier.

However, when Diego would come home from his business, he would hold the two black babies in his hands and weigh them. Then, a bit later; he would do the same with the twins. After doing this, he would tell Mariana —as his wife was named— "Mariana, the wetnurse slaves are giving the black babies more milk than they are giving our sons. One of these days, I'm going to be so mad that I'm going to strangle those black babies."

Mariana would desperately reply: "For God's sake, Diego, don't say that! It's both against God's law and human law what you are saying." He would angrily fire back: "I don't give a damn about religion and all that nonsense! I'm going to kill them one day."

One day, he came and killed the poor black babies. All the mothers could do at that moment was to sob and lament because they were slaves. However, one Sunday morning while the couple had gone to Mass at Our Lady of Charity Church, Encarnación and Tomasa killed the twins along with another child and threw the bodies in the courtyard's well.

The couple's oldest child, an 11-year-old girl, escaped to her uncle's home, carrying one of her brothers. Before the authorities arrived, Encarnación and Tomasa tried to commit suicide by throwing themselves into the well. Once the authorities arrived, they got them out of the well alive, arrested them, took them to jail and then to court.

One can imagine Diego's community reputation when the court decided not to condemn the two black slaves to death. One was given a light prison sentence, and the other one was given a few lashes. From then on, Mariana locked herself in her bedroom and barred the door so that Diego couldn't come in.

Every afternoon, he would pound on the door, frantically yelling: "Mariana, open the door! Open the damn door!" But she wouldn't and people began to sing a song around town which went like this:

> On Sunday Morning
> Two black slaves
> Killed three little angels
> With a knife they made
> They killed three little angels
> It's treason, it's treason
> But Diego also had no reason
> It happened on Sunday morning
> Now, the whole town is mourning.

In that home there were a lot of shackles, bayonets, and other artifacts. It was called "The Home Where the Crime was Committed." It was located in La Caridad District, right on Libertad Avenue. People always admonished us: "Don't go there!" No one wanted to live there because they were afraid Diego would come out of this grave and attack them. People used to say that Diego used all of those artifacts to force his pregnant slaves to climb the coconut trees in his plantation to gather coconuts. Those trees were really tall and it was dangerous to climb them.

The rumors about the artifacts and the tree climbing weren't true. The real story is that the home had been converted into a small Spanish garrison in 1895 and when the war ended all of these artifacts remained there. They were probably used to torture some of the patriots when they were caught.

I remember we used to sneak through the back of the home and play with them. One time, though, one of the kids got hurt playing with those things there, but we made up a story so we wouldn't get punished for going to "The Home Where the Crime was Committed."

BLACKS, CHINESE, SPANISH, AND HAITIANS

JOSEFINA PÉREZ: Relations between blacks and whites in Cienfuegos were very good. Blacks and whites were treated the same. Houses were rented to blacks, just as they were rented to whites. They lived next to each other as good neighbors and they got along great.

One thing, though, in Cienfuegos, whites had their own social clubs and blacks also had their own separate social clubs. The black social club in Cienfuegos was the Minerva Social Club. They held great events at that club.

CELESTINO SUÁREZ: Cienfuegos was the city that least discriminated against blacks in Cuba. However, in the park, the whites strolled right in the center of the park and the blacks outside the center. One time, blacks tried to stroll where the whites strolled, shots were fired - and all hell broke loose. As a matter of fact, Joseíto, the candy maker, who was black – well - someone shot his daughter in the butt.

FÉLIX MEDINILLA: There was a very good central park in Trinidad, but the whites strolled this way, and the blacks strolled the other way. Then, one day, Dr. Alfredo Zayas[84], President of the Cuban Republic, decreed that everyone had the same rights and that there wasn't going to be any separation in the parks. Additionally, he said that if people didn't want to abide by the law,

---

[84] Alfredo Zayas y Alfonso (1861-1934). Cuban erudite who was President of Cuba from 1921 until 1925. Born in Havana on February 21, 1861, he died in said city, on April 11, 1934. Although the Cuban Constitution of 1901 prohibited any form of discrimination, the custom of blacks strolling in parks, separately from whites, continued until after dictator Machado's fall.

they would not be allowed in the parks. I can assure that this is a true story.

CARLOS MONTERO: Cuba didn't have the racial tensions that exist in the United States. Sure, there was a difference between educated blacks and uneducated blacks but there was also a difference between educated whites and white trash. Blacks had their own social clubs, and so did the whites. No one messed around with the social clubs.

LORENZO ZEQUEIRA: Relations between blacks and whites in Cuba were very cordial. First of all, I want to make it perfectly clear that I belonged to a black social club to which the most illustrious blacks in Havana belonged. However, whites could also be members if they met the same requirements as blacks. The social club that I'm talking about was the "Atenas Social Club."

I'm someone who tells it like it is, but before doing that, I examine things, and analyze things. To me, a black who is decent - I'm black - has the same rights as a white who is decent. I have danced at ball dances at the Hotel Nacional, [85] and the Centro Gallego, [86] and I've never been discriminated against.

If there was discrimination in Cuba, it was because of a certain town's tradition or something like that. It wasn't racial at all. For example, at Vidal Park in Santa Clara where I once went, I saw that whites strolled in one place, mulattoes in another place, and blacks still, in another place. It was just a tradition among the three groups. It was a tradition, so I can't say it was discrimination.

MARIO VEGA: In Cuba, blacks weren't demeaned. I used to go dancing at different places and whites, blacks and mulattoes were

---

[85] The Hotel Nacional still exists today and throughout history, it has been Cuba's most famous hotel. It opened in 1930.

[86] Spanish social club in Havana built in 1914 and noted for its opulent architectural style.

there. I used to dance with blacks and mulattoes because I'm a man without prejudices. I have very good friends who are black and they love me a lot, and I've gone to their places to have dinner with them. I have great admiration for blacks because one of the greatest figures in Cuban history was Antonio Maceo y Grajales. Additionally, there's a Cuban saying that "In Cuba the one who doesn't have Congolese ancestry, has Carabalí[87] ancestry."

VÍCTOR VEGA CEBALLOS: In Camagüey, during Spanish colonial times, black slaves were household servants and were given the master's last name. In the countryside, on the other hand, they were given the plantation's name as their last name.

Society in Camagüey was very stratified, even among the black population. For example, people of color had different social clubs: two for blacks and two for mulattoes. In one of the black social clubs, membership was based on professions like teachers, doctors, lawyers, etc. The other was for blacks who were poor such as stevedores, street sweepers and others in lesser professions. The "aristocratic" one was named "Maceo," while the plebeian one was named "Victoria." The irony was that "Victoria" had a better building and better furnishings than "Maceo." There was the same stratification in the mulatto community, but, one of the social clubs had a funny inscription which stated the following: "This Social Club is for those who are mulattoes or look like mulattoes."

ENRIQUE CASERO: We never distinguished between blacks and whites. Nowadays, I go to see black friends here in the United States. They've been my friends since the times we had the farm in San Luis and I love them dearly.

I've always believed that those who criticize blacks do so because they probably have black blood and they resent that,

---

[87] Ethnic group which inhabits the Western Niger Delta in present-day Nigeria. Many of the slaves brought to Cuba were of Carabalí origin.

which is totally wrong. I once had a friend who was always criticizing blacks and couldn't stand them. Well, years later, it was found out that the damn guy had black blood. That was the reason for his prejudice.

MANUEL GARCÍA IGLESIAS: Blacks and whites got along very well. In Sagua, where I spent my childhood, there was no separation between blacks and whites. There were no ghettoes like there are here. That didn't exist. However, I do have to acknowledge that there was racial discrimination when it came to jobs. For example, in banks and railroad companies, there were no blacks in managerial positions. Perhaps, it was because the railroad company was British and the banks were foreign owned. In other job categories, there was no discrimination. To be prejudiced is not to be Cuban.

ANA AURORA RECIO: Relations between blacks and whites in Camagüey were very good. We were eight children in our family and the eight of us were nursed by black wet nurses. In our times, it was customary for children of well-to-do families to be nursed by black female servants. We simply adored them, and our parents taught us to love them. They would always tell us: "They are your second mothers; you have to love them."

HORTENSIA LÓPEZ: There has never been racial prejudice in Cuba. In our home, there was a servant named Mamá Isabel. She was a heavyset black lady who helped to raise us and for us, that black lady was like our mother. She was a family member.

MARÍA ELBA GONZÁLEZ: In our home there was an ex-slave. Her name was Rosalía Abreu because the Abreus had been the masters. She raised my grandmother. She was the only person who used the *tú* familiar form with my grandmother, because with my grandmother, everyone had to use the *usted* polite form. She would even boss my grandmother! She had a great sense of humor. I remember her; and she was over 100 years old.

I knew another one called "La Cundina." She was an elderly black woman. She was the one who raised me. She took care of me. She dressed me, she took me to school and fixed my lunch. She did everything for me. The last time I saw her was in 1940 she was very old. I loved her very much.

There were numerous black servants at our home because when the family-owned "Dolores" sugar mill was dismantled, a number of blacks whose livelihood depended on the sugar mill, came to my grandmother asking her: "Lady Rosita, what are we going to do now? What's going to become of us?" My grandmother bought them a *cuartería*[88] in the town's outskirts, placed all of them there and told them: "No one is going to go hungry and if anyone of you gets hungry, you come to my home to eat." There were large families in that group, and some of them, while they were getting settled, came to my grandmother's home to eat.

VÍCTOR VEGA CEBALLOS: In Spanish colonial times, slavery was not as violent and sedicious, and not as ruthless as it was in other colonial powers. Of course, abuses were committed and even in the years of the Cuban Republic there was a certain form of *apartheid*. At Camagüey's Central Park, for example, blacks were not allowed until after Machado's fall.

Regarding white and black relations in Cuba, I have an anecdote as to what happened to a Cuban black politician, and it's an amusing one and yet, ironic. In Cuba, it was customary in places where goat meat is eaten, to invite friends to eat "stolen goat." The goat meat that was going to be served had to come from a stolen goat. It couldn't come from a goat which was a gift or from one which was purchased; it had to be from a stolen goat. One day, in the middle of a political campaign, Prisciliano Piedra, who was a black congressman from Matanzas Province was wearing a pair of baggy pants known as "pantalones con bueyes" because its label had a pair of oxen, stretching the pants, trying to

---

[88] String of one room dwellings generally occupied by low income individuals

break them and they couldn't do it. The label was a marketing tool to prove the pants' strength. He was also wearing a shirt that looked more like a costume than a shirt. In other words, he looked like a bum, rather than a congressman.

Right in the middle of the campaign he told a number of friends: "Let's make a goat stew." One of the guys said: "Let's do that, let's go and steal a goat." So, they went to the town's outskirts, saw a goat in a yard and while Prisciliano was grabbing it, the poor creature started bellowing. Suddenly, people came out and summoned the police. The police came, arrested them, and took them to the police station.

The group arrived at the police station and the officer pointed out Prisciliano to the police chief and said: "I'm bringing this black dude to you; he was trying to steal a goat." The chief was writing a note and said: "He has to be black because all blacks are a bunch of thieves." He kept on writing without looking at Prisciliano and asked him what was his name. Prisciliano replied: "I'm Prisciliano Piedra." The chief, without looking at Prisciliano answered, saying: "So, you are named Prisciliano Piedra, just like the congressman's name." Prisciliano replied: "No, I'm Congressman Prisciliano Piedra!" The chief looked at Prisciliano and Prisciliano let him have it by saying: "I'm Prisciliano Piedra. You didn't recognize me because of the way I'm dressed. In fact, you didn't even look at me. Now would you please continue saying all those things you were saying about blacks? I'll like to hear them again so that I can find out how blacks are treated when they are brought to your station." The poor chief almost had a heart attack!

MARIO VEGA: The Chinese in Cuba solved many problems. The Chinese were very hard-working. The Chinese lived altogether in one place. They lived like packed sardines and they were very skinny.

Many Chinese owned dry-cleaning businesses and would dry clean laundry cheaply. Many of them had fried food stands where one could eat cheaply too. Thanks to the Chinese, Cubans could eat for pennies.

Zanja Street - that's where Chinatown was located. Over there, one could go to their fruit stands, and drink the best pineapple and orange juice is in the world. The Chinese were very respectful and law-abiding citizens. There were never problems with the Chinese. In Cuba, there was the famous phrase of "There has never been a Chinese traitor in Cuban history."

CEFERINO GARCÍA: The Chinese are very grateful people. When the Chinese would see that one would treat them nicely, they would become friends for life. They, for example, had a very well organized community in Sagua. They were very adaptable and learned Spanish very well. Some of them were great produce farmers. Every day they came to the central market with basketfuls of produce. There were other Chinese who were grocery store owners and did very well.

JOSEFINA PÉREZ: Many Chinese in Cienfuegos sold food. They would put the food inside huge cans. The cans had well-lit charcoal to keep the food warm. They would put those cans at the end of a large pole and carry the pole with the cans on their shoulders. I don't know how a skinny Chinese could carry all that food in those cans because they weighed a lot.

I remember that when one would see a Chinese coming down the street with those cans, one would come out with plates and bowls to buy the food they had available. The food was delicious and was hot because of the charcoal. That was a long time ago. I was a little child then, but now I'm 92 years old.

RODOLOFO SOTOLONGO: In Colón, there were Chinese who had a produce farm. Actually, my family owned the land, so they were our tenant farmers. They grew all kinds of vegetables. They would give us some of their crops, and the rest were sold in Colón.

They lived right there on our land. People said they smoked opium in bamboo pipes, but I never saw them doing it. However, I know for a fact that there was a brave Chinese guy who fought in Cuba's War of Independence and his name was José Bó.

CEFERINO GARCÍA: I'm Spanish but I emigrated to Cuba just like two brothers of mine had previously done. Naturally, my brother sponsored me to go to Cuba, fleeing the war in Morocco [89].

In Spain, I had a vision of Cuba from what I had heard from Austurians living in Cuba. They would come to visit relatives in Asturias. In life, there are two sides to a coin and while I was in Spain, I was seeing only one. However, when I arrived in Cuba, I saw the other side of the coin.

The first place I saw in Cuba was Tiscornia[90]. I was taken there because someone from the Spanish liner *Alfonso XII* had a contagious illness. So, we went to Tiscornia for checkups, in order to prevent an epidemic breakout. I liked it there because it was at that place where I first tasted the guava paste and other Cuban delicacies. I liked it there very much.

I was in Tiscornia for three days until the doctors cleared us to leave. Outside, I saw trucks unloading oranges and other fruits. When I saw that I said to myself: "Oh, my God, this place looks like where I was raised; there are so many fruits here!"

Later on, we went to Sagua and lived there until October 10, 1966, when I left because of the Castro regime. Leaving Sagua was very hard because of all the years I spent there. I went to Sagua, sponsored by my older brothers and started working at the same place where they worked. It was a store, and Antonio García was its owner. It was located on 7 Colón Street, right on General Lee's corner. It was a general store which sold food,

---

[89] From 1893 until 1926 Spain on and off fought a series of colonial wars against tribesmen in Morocco. Many of the Spanish casualties in those wars were young Spanish recruits.

[90] Immigrant processing center in Cuba.

tools, clothing, shoes and many other items. It also had a bakery named "La Bayamesa."

We lived right in the store and slept on cots behind the doors. In 1922, two bedrooms were added upstairs and we slept there. It was much nicer sleeping in those rooms. There were tough years, full of sacrifices, but we made progress in Cuba.

During the first years I was in Cuba, there were many Spanish in the wholesale and retail businesses. Later on, Cubans began to replace the Spanish and they did very well. Undoubtedly, there may be one or two individuals who differ from my opinion, but as for me, there is no one more similar to a Spanish than a Cuban and vice versa. One can mistake a Cuban for a Spanish and a Spanish for a Cuban.

It's true that at times Cubans referred to all the Spanish as "Gallegos" (Galicians), but that wasn't derogatory. It was more of a term of endearment. I don't think that any Spanish got mad about being called "Gallego."

CARLOS MONTERO: Relations between Spanish and Cubans were excellent! There wasn't any animosity whatsoever. The Spanish who lived in Cuba were more Cuban than the Cubans themselves. Many Spanish advanced very well economically because they were hard workers.

The Spanish were unique. They took care of their own quite well. After being in Cuba, the Spanish store owner would bring his nephew from Spain, and the latter, after a few years, would become the store owner. So, he began sweeping the floor and ended up being the store owner.

The Spanish adapted well in Cuba and became educated in Cuba. They had lots of organizations, ranging from social clubs to mutual aid entities. Their hospitals were magnificent and so were their organizations. They were good and active people.

RODOLFO SOTOLONGO: The Cubans and the Spanish got along very well. Even during the War of Independence, relations were good. When Cuba became independent, relations remained very good because there has always been a strong bond between them.

Peace and friendship, as General Máximo Gómez foretold, reigned. In my hometown, 95% of the businesses were owned by the Spanish. They were well-liked in my hometown. Many of them married Cuban ladies and their love for Cuba was the same as those who had been born on the island.

VÍCTOR VEGA CEBALLOS: In Camagüey, Spanish immigrants had difficulties trying to get married because Camagüeyan women were not too keen about marrying them. Even during Spanish colonial times, they were picky. They would marry a Spanish guy who was a captain, a colonel or a general, but an average Spanish guy, no way!

Camagüeyans were very special, and tended to marry within the family. In Camagüey, there was the following saying: "Better than an outsider, an insider, better than an insider, someone from your hometown, better than someone from your hometown, someone from your neighborhood, better than someone from your neighborhood, someone from your family."

There was a conflict in my family. My maternal grandmother only had one sister and one brother because the Spanish authorities had killed the rest of her brothers in 1851. Her sister, Aunt Cheché, on the other hand, was more Spanish than Pelayo[91]. She hated Cubans, and was always telling my sisters not to marry Cubans because according to her, Cubans were good for nothing, lazy, and all they did was to stand on street corners telling jokes and stories. She said my sisters should marry Spanish men because they were real men.

My aunt was an interesting person. She had been married three times. First, she had been married to a Cuban. The man died young from a heart attack and apparently, he had mistreated

---

[91] Pelayo (685-737). Founder of the Kingdom of Asturias, Spain, he initiated the Spanish Reconquest in 717 against the Muslim occupiers.

her. Afterwards, she married Spanish high-ranking military officers. When she returned from Spain after her third husband had died, she raised a mulatto child named Victoriano Luquero. Since her last husband had been a high ranking Spanish military officer in Camagüey, she ordered a Spanish military officer uniform made for Victoriano. Whenever there was a Spanish Army military parade, there was Aunt Cheché and Victoriano, viewing the parade from the stands.

FÉLIX MEDINILLA: My godfather was a Catalonian named Isidro Rodríguez. Even though I was black and he was white, he was my godfather. He knew my father during the War of Independence, and although he was Spanish and my father was Cuban, he told my father: "I'm going to be your firstborn son's godfather." I was the first and only one.

He treated me nicely and when I used to go to his wholesale business, he was very kind. He's probably dead by now, because that was a long time ago. I have nothing bad to say about the Spanish.

MANUEL GARCÍA IGLESIAS: Relations between Cubans and Spanish were very good. There were hardly any tensions among them. The only possible one was that Cubans felt a bit discriminated against because in Spanish-owned businesses, it was customary for owners to bring their nephews from Spain; thus, it was difficult for Cubans to work in such businesses.

However, in 1933 that practice ended with the enactment of the Fifty Percent Law[92] which decreed that 50% of a business's workforce had to be made up of Cubans. That law ended the "importation" of Spanish nephews and ended that labor problem. There was a complete bonding of Cubans and Spanish. I never had any bad feelings towards the Spanish.

---

[92] Its official name was the Nationalization Work Law. It was passed in 1933 under the administration of Cuban Interim President Ramón Grau San Martín.

ERNIQUE CASERO: There were lots of Haitians in Oriente Province. My father had a Haitian friend named Antoine. The man had about nine Haitians in his crew, cleaning my father's farm fields. He was a good, decent man, who gave money to my father for safekeeping.

One day, he decided to return to Haiti and told my father: "Don Paco, you've been very good to me. I'm going to Haiti because it has been a long time since I've been there. If I ever return, I know that you will give me that money that you've been keeping." He never returned, but my father kept that money for him, as promised. That's the kind of friendship there was between the Haitians and my father.

FELIPE ROLOFF: When there was the sugar boom, many Haitians came to work in the sugar industry around Morón[93]. At one point there were around 200 cane cutters in our farm. No Cuban wanted to be a cane cutter; so Haitians had to be imported to work in the cane fields.

The Haitians did not work at all in the sugar mill. They were the ones who cut cane and cleaned the fields. It was hard work using a hoe for planting and a machete for cutting. There were no cane cutting machines. Everything was done by hand and the Haitians did it. There was a total separation between Haitians and Cubans. None of them visited Cuban homes and none of the Cubans visited them. At that time, Haitians were very backward and there was a total separation. They had that Haitian-African religion. I remember that when there was a *bembé* in a farm, I would go. I just wanted to see and learn. I remember I used to go with my brothers. They treated us well because we were the farm owners. They would offer us food to eat, but we wouldn't eat it. I remember them decapitating chickens and goats, dressing them and making stews full of goat meat and all

---

[93] Haitian immigration to Cuba reached its zenith from 1913 until 1920 as a result of an increase in production in the Cuban sugar industry. It continued on a minor scale until the 1950s

kinds of vegetables. One of them would stand at one end with an ore mixing all of that stuff, and another one would be doing something at the other end. They sweat a lot with all that heat.

The Haitians' living conditions were horrible, so I guess they had to do something to enjoy themselves. There was heavy drinking at their *bembés*. They drank *aguardiente* which was the cheapest drink costing about 25 cents a liter.

There was also a lot of fighting among them because they were three or four Haitian women for those 200 Haitian men and they would fight for them. I think that Haitian immigration was heavy in Cuba until the Fifty Percent Law went into effect.

Víctor Vega, c. 1970s
(Courtesy of Eduardo Febles)

VÍCTOR VEGA CEBALLOS: In Oriente Province, there are many well-educated Haitians and many rich Haitians. They had brought their capital to Cuba and acquired coffee plantations. They were excellent coffee growers.

Haiti is a short distance from Cuba so when Mister Sterling, a Haitian, left Haiti, he brought his sugar mill on barges to Cuba. He was the first important member of those immigrants in Cuba. There are descendants of that man in Cuba, or at least of his slaves. All of his slaves' last name was Sterlano.

There was also a French immigration to Cuba, although not many of them came to Camagüey. However, there were many French that came to Matanzas. They were from Louisiana. Cienfuegos, by the way, in Las Villas Province, was founded by the French from Louisiana. Douclé was the one who founded Cienfuegos and there is a street in that city that bears his name. Dauclé was a French military officer who was a general in the Spanish Army.

THE CUBAN *GUAJIRO*[94]

FELIPE ROLOFF: In Cuba, there were different types of *guajiros* and I say this with authority because I was born in the countryside, lived in the countryside, and I have been all over Cuba. The *guajiro* from Pinar del Río Province was very backward and very poor. There was a lack of transportation in that province and many of them lived in the hill country. They just lived a subsistence type of life. In Oriente Province, the *guajiro's* situation was similar because there were high mountains in that province. However, the *guajiro* in Havana Province was more advanced because transportation was no problem; with Havana being the Cuban capital.

Generally, the *guajiro* was a very noble and humble individual. The one thing the *guajiro* would not tolerate was messing around with him and pissing him off. If a *guajiro* was provoked, he would react violently and pull out his machete. He could kill anyone with a machete stroke. The *guajiro* had a great sense of personal honor and the Cuban countryside was known for machete duels.

Another *guajiro* trait was shyness. For example, if one wanted to talk to the head of the family, all of the family would leave and hide. By the way, in Cuba, when a child was very shy, people would tell him: "Don't act like a *guajiro*."

HORTENSIA LÓPEZ: The Cuban *guajiros* were generally very noble and very hard-working. Among them, there was neither thievery nor the crazy things that we see today. There was no evil among them. They were simply good people.

---

[94] The word is used in Cuba for peasant. Although the etymology of the word is debatable, it's probably derived from Taino-Arawak meaning "Lord."

My godmother had a farm up the road from El Caney. It was close to El Rodeo, a little village. When one visited the *guajiros* there, they would make fresh coffee for the visitors and were very nice to them. The coffee was delicious because they roasted and grounded it. They would roast it in a huge pot and grounded it with a huge oarlike mortar.

MARIO VEGA: I was a traveling salesman in Cuba and I know Cuba very well. Being a traveling salesman gave me the opportunity to meet many *guajiros*. They were good people, gentle and kind. They were without malice, and very courteous. When one visited a *guajiro's* bohío, they would give you everything they had. Sure, they were uneducated and the majority of them were illiterate, but they were kindhearted. Unfortunately, in Cuba, some people took advantage of the *guajiros*.

I would also visit the sugar mills' *bateyes* to sell goods to the mill's company store. The store sold goods to the *guajiros* on credit at exorbitant interest rates during the off season and they had to pay the company store during the *zafra* (grinding season). This meant that the *guajiros* were in constant debt to the company store.

I used to travel through the countryside and I would see the *guajiros*, full of wrinkles with calluses all over their hands from cutting cane or plowing the fields. They were men in their 30s or 40s, but they looked like they were in their 60s, with their faces all sundrenched. It was pathetic seeing them and seeing how quickly they aged. It seems as if they had never gotten a fair shake. Yet, they remained silent, never complaining and always doing their jobs.

The truth must be told. The truth may not be pleasant but it's still the truth, and if I'm rubbing salt on the wound, so be it. Cuba was a very rich land; no one should have gone hungry there or just making ends meet. But, it happened to the *guajiros*. I am telling the truth and I can verify what I'm saying any time.

MARÍA ELBA GONZÁLEZ: I know the *guajiro* way of life quite well because there were many *guajiros* living near my hometown.

One of their most important traits was that of building a *cobija* (palm thatched schack). The *cobija* was built with *jiquí*[95] beams, because *jiquí* is a very strong type of wood and since it was strong, the *guajiro* wanted his *cobija* to last a lifetime. Afterwards, the roof would be thatched with sabel palm fronds because they have long and wide fronds. I don't know how they thatched the roof, but I know that water never got through these fronds. The *cobija* was totally waterproof.

    As to the floor, it had a dirt floor, but the dirt was covered with thick ashes and that floor was like cement. In fact, it could be swept with a broom. Regarding the walls, they were made out of royal palm wood. The *cobija* also had windows, but of course, there were no glass windows.

    The kitchen was outside, so there was no danger of the *cobija* catching fire. As far as the bathroom was concerned, there might had been an outhouse or they simply went to a banana grove and did their things there. The *cobjia* had no lights so the *guajiro* had to use kerosene lamps called *chismosas*.

    The *guajiro* had four important possessions: his *cobija*, his horse, his guitar and his *taburete*. The *guajiros* knew how to throw a *guateque* (country dance). One would see the *guajiras* nicely dressed in those *guateques*. Their *guateque* dresses were white with red polka dots and laces. They were beautiful! At times, the *guajiras* would also put flowers in their hair.

    The *guateques* were normally on Sunday afternoons and feastdays. Their *puntos guajiros* (country songs) were played with a guitar, a clef, and a *tres* which was a three-string instrument, smaller than the guitar. In the *guateques*, there were *décima* contests. They were something else to see and hear because a player had to improvise, play and sing a *décima* rapidly and his rival had to reply in the same fashion immediately. Wow! The *décimas gua-*

---

[95] According to srouces, *jiquí* is a Cuban hardwood tree, resistant to moisture.

jiras are beautiful. Ignacio Cervantes[96] was the forerunner of the "Guajira" which is a Cuban type of music describing the Cuban landscape and the *guajiro* way of life. What a wonderful musician! One of his most beautiful compositions is precisely called "La Guajira" and it goes like this:

> I have a treasure
> In my modest *bohío*
> She reigns over it
> She is the woman I love so much
> I sing my melancholic song
> Accompanied by my lira (lyre)
> What I have in my *bohío* inspires me to sing
> The reminiscences from the war
> My country's flag
> And my love for my *guajira*.

RODOLFO SOTOLONGO: The Cuban *guajiro's* traditional dance is the *zapateo* (shoe tapping dance). I used to see it dance at the *guateques*. A couple would always dance the *zapateo*. The *guajiro* would be dressed with his *guayabera*, his straw hat and a red kerchief covering his neck. The *guajira* would wear her beautiful dress and would have a handkerchief in her hands.

The *zapateo* was a beautiful, but difficult dance. There were two ways to dance it: there was the *punteado* which consisted of short steps using the tip and back of the shoes and the *escobillado* which consisted of sliding the shoes on the floor and making broomlike motions on the floor.

The *zapateo* was played with a *tres* or a guitar, a *guiro* (gourd), a clef, and sometimes an accordion. The *taburete's* hide was used to provide percussion. The *zapateo* was similar to the Argentine gauchos' (cowhands) dance. All of these dances came

---

[96] Ignacio Cervantes (1847-1905). Known for the Cubanness of his musical compositions, he was a Cuban patriot, musician and composer. He was born in Havana, on July 31, 1847 and died there, on April 30, 1905.

from Spain, and were somewhat modified in the colonies. The majority of them were Andalusian in origin because there were many Andalusians that came with Columbus to the New World. Columbus left from the Andalusian port of Palos de Moguer and the majority of his sailors were from Seville and Huelva in Andalucía.

CEFERINO GARCÍA: I not only went to *guateques* but I was also a bartender in the big *guateques* like the ones on *Sábado de Gloria*. I did that because at times we would have a good client come to our store and say to us: "I'm going to promote a big *guateque*, can you be one of our sponsors?" So, we would pay for the musicians, donate beer, refreshments and sweets. That way, our client could make some money. We did that for free, as a token of appreciation for being a loyal customer throughout the year.

The *Sábado de Gloría guateque* was much more than a dance. The *guajiros* not only enjoyed the dancing but also the horseback tournaments. They would ride at full speed trying to get the lance through a ring. I enjoyed watching those tournaments there a lot. Those *guajiros* seemed to be flying through the air riding those horses. It was really fantastic!

MANUEL GARCÍA IGLESIAS: I used to attend *guateques*. Over, in the countryside, one didn't have to wear a suit to go to these dances. The *guajiros* would dress in their *guayaberas*. Actually, they weren't *guayaberas*, but rather *trocheras*. They were similar to the *guayaberas*, but its clothing material was thicker and they were beige-colored.

There was heavy drinking at those places. The most popular beverages were beer, rum and *aguardiente* (firewater). Sometimes they would add honey, basil and mint to the *aguardiente*. Mojitos would also be prepared there. There were also all kinds of sodas, but the most popular were "Champagne Sport" and "Purita" lemon soda both made and bottled in Sagua. As far as food was concerned, there were all kinds of food. For example, there was goat stew, roast pork, tamales, empanadas, and other typical Cuban dishes.

Those dances were picturesque; however, at times, a fight would break out because the *guajiros* were very jealous people. I witnessed two or three fights at these *guateques*. At times, those fights got out of hand and ended in machete duels, but I never got to see any of them.

ENRIQUE CASERO: The most important thing for a *guajiro* was to build his *bohío*. As a matter of fact, many of them would build their *bohíos* before meeting their future brides. I remember Mengo, a *guajiro* who was a *desmochador* (royal palm tree trimmer). He was a hard worker but he was a knucklehead. He was a master at building *bohíos*.

One day, Mengo built a beautiful bohío, because he had fallen in love with a *guajira* whose last name was Plutín. She didn't know that he was in love with her. So, he came to where her family lived and told her: "Hey, I want you to come along with me, I want you to be my wife." She replied: "But Mengo, you never told me that you were in love with me." Mengo, then, told her that if she didn't come along with him, he was going to burn the *bohío*. The *guajira* refused to come along with him and that same evening, he burned the *bohío*. I don't know, but people say that when a *guajira* rejects a *guajiro*, the latter burns the *bohío*. I felt sorry for Mengo. He worked so hard building that *bohío* just to burn it to the ground in a single evening.

I think the world's hardest job is that of being a *desmochador*. He had to climb a royal palm tree, put a rope under the *palmiche* (fruit of the royal palm tree) bunch and pull the rope with all of his strength so that the *palmiche* bunch would fall on top of the oxcart. A *desmochador* risked his life for 10 or 15 cents he received for each palm tree.

After cutting off the bunches and taking them to our farm we would put the *palmiche* to dry for 10 to 15 days. Once the *palmiche* was dried, one couldn't even walk on top of them because they were hotter than hell and they itched a lot. We used to give *palmiche* to our pigs. That was the way we fattened our pigs. If pigs eat *palmiche*, they produce lots of lard. The *guajiros* used to give lots of *palmiche* mixed with *boniatos* to their pigs. Giving them *palmiche* was much better than giving them pig feed.

One thing that *guajiros* loved was cockfighting. Well, not only *guajiros* enjoyed cockfighting, but many people did. My brother, Aurelio, used to raise gamecocks. The best gamecocks were the Spanish ones. They were better than the Cuban gamecocks because the Cubans were often mixed and the Spanish ones were thoroughbreds. The Cuban gamecocks, at times, would start running when pecked or struck with a spur in a cockfight and many would start flying the coop. That's why in Cuba we have the expression: "He flew the coop" to mean that someone suddenly left the place because things were looking bad for him.

Enrique Casero with wife Denyse, 1979
(Courtesy of Dr. Enrique Casero Jr.)

PIMPS AND HUMAN TRAFFICKING

MARIO VEGA: In practically every town in Cuba there was a *cuartería* because if the poor didn't have a place to go, they would go to a *cuartería,* and tried to live by their wits. It was nice going to a *cuartería*. One would experience typical Cuban happy times such as drinking beer and rum, eating fried pork chunks and dancing *rumba*[97] and *mambo*.[98] The majority of the people living there were black and mulattoes, but once in awhile there were whites there too. I loved going to the *cuarterías*. There was heavy drinking there and it was enjoyable.

At times, there were fights in the *cuarterías* because *chulos* (pimps) would frequent them. If a *chulo* saw his woman with another *chulo* there would be a fight. He would pull out his switchblade and cut the other man's face in the middle of the street. I saw many *chulos* on Crespo Street because that street was famous for its whores and *chulos.*

Generally, a *chulo* dressed nicely. He had three or four whores working for him. He would come at the end of the day to collect from them what he thought was due to him. The Cuban *chulo* was a real *chulo* unlike the American *chulo* who is really shitty. I remember seeing *chulos* in Cuba ever since I was a kid. Probably, there is more prostitution in Cuba today than there is in

---

[97] Style of folk dancing originally developed by the poor in Cuba during the second half of the 19th century. There have been many ramifications of the rumba since the 20th century.

[98] Cuban dance invented during the 1930s which became popular in the 1940s and 1950s throughout Cuba and North America. Mambo's biggest personality in Mexico and the United States was Cuban bandleader Dámaso Pérez Prado (1916-1989) who was known as "The King of Mambo."

the United States, but I don't know if there are *chulos* there today.

CELESTINO SUÁREZ: The children couldn't go to the red-light district, but I used to go with our butcher shop delivery guy. If a policeman would come by, I used to say: "I'm here helping the delivery man." I used to go there to see what whores looked like.

At that time, there were men who were *chulos*, but they didn't need to be *chulos*. There was Juan González, for example; his father was filthy rich, so he didn't need to be a *chulo*. There was another one named Paco. He was always all dressed up with the most elegant suit and a flower on his lapel. Everyone knew he was a *chulo* but he didn't need to be one because he was rich. He had three or four women working for him and yet, he was a member of the *Liceo* and the Casino Español.

In Cuba, there were *chulos* but there was also human trafficking, targeting foreign white women. I'm talking about 1918 or so. It was a business and those involved in that business would go to France and talk to nice-looking French young ladies and would tell them: "We are going to take you as servants to Cuba and you are going to earn 60 *pesos* a month." Obviously, the young ladies said yes because 60 *pesos* a month at that time was a respectable sum of money. So, they would start them as servants and send them to Cuba in ocean liners. All of that cost a lot of money.

Once they arrived in Havana, things appeared to be nice. The young ladies would stay for a few days in a nice place and suddenly, they would come to the place and say to them: "Now, you have to pay us for all of the expenses." That's where all hell would break loose because the poor young ladies had no money. So, those bastards would give them to a *chulo* who had them as his prostitutes and both the *chulo* and the traffickers made their money off them.

Many of those young ladies later went to work at brothels specializing in rich clients. I was friends with one of these young ladies and she already had some 20,000 *pesos* in bank savings. For every *peso* she collected from prostitution, she had to give half to the brothel. However, she could keep the tips for herself. She was so beautiful and so attractive. That's what made her rich clients give her lots of money.

BANDITS

CELESTINO SUÁREZ: During Spanish colonial days there were many bandits throughout Cuba. There was one nicknamed "Cayito",[99] who was a real tough one and was never captured. Also, around Camagüey, there was Francisco Marty,[100] who was a slave smuggler. My father used to tell me that my grandfather who was the police chief in town during Spanish colonial times, once captured a bandit.

According to the story, the bandit was spotted, but ran away and climbed a tree. He had been in that tree for hours and people were expecting him to come down, but he wouldn't. My grandfather then arrived and said to him: "Hey, man! Come down! Here is a cigar for you." Well, he was stupid because he came down and my grandfather arrested him.

RODOLFO SOTOLONGO: The most famous bandit in Cuban history was Manuel García.[101] He was sort of like the Cuban Robin Hood because he stole from the rich to give to the poor. They called him "The King of Cuban Countryside." The Spanish Civil Guard which was the equivalent of the future Cuban Rural Guard

---

[99] Famous bandit from Las Villas Province who joined the Cuban Liberation Army during the War of Cuban Independence, reaching the rank of Lieutenant Colonel. He became a defector and was killed by patriots' forces. His real name was Cándido Alvarez.

[100] Famous slave trafficker and smuggler during Spanish colonial times in Cuba. He operated out of Las Villas, not Camagüey. Spanish authorities killed him in 1866.

[101] Manuel Garcia (1851-1895). Undoubtedly, the most famous bandit in Cuban folklore. He was born in Alacranes, Matanzas Province, on February 1, 1851. Troubles with Spanish authorities made him seek refuge in the countryside and turned to banditry. Apparently, he was killed while trying to join the Cuban Liberation Army either on February 23 or 24, 1895.

could neither capture nor kill him. He operated out of Havana Province and part of Matanzas Province.

On February 24, 1895, Manuel García got killed. He was going to join Juan Gualberto Gómez[102] in Ibarra, Matanzas Province to fight the Spanish. García along with his followers was going to meet Gómez, but he was ambushed at El Seborucal, near the town of Ceiba Mocha, Matanzas Province, and was assassinated there. Supposedly he was killed by Spanish regular army troops. However, there is another version that a group of landowners had killed him because he was extorting money from them. Apparently, Manuel García was killed while trying to join the Cuban patriots in their quest for Cuban independence. He was so popular that he was the subject of many stories, including the short poem that went like this:

> Manuel García says
> That if they don't give him what he wants
> He'll pull down
> The policemens' pants
> Manuel García says
> That if they don't give him *centenes*
> He'll derail the *trenes* (trains)

In the area around Colón, right after the War of Independence, there were a few bandits but once the Rural Guard Corps was established, it eliminated them. There were some famous bandits around the area prior to the War of Independence, though. There was one who later joined the Cuban Liberation Army whose last name was Matagás[103]. Still there was another one called "El

---

[102] Juan Gualberto Gómez (1854-1934). Cuban War of Independence patriot and one of José Martí'sprincipal collaborators. After Cuban Independence, he was one of the most important figures in Cuban political history. He was born in Sabanilla del Encomendador, Matanzas Province, on July 12, 1854, and died in Havana, on March 5, 1934.

[103] José Álvarez Ortega, famous as"Matagás," was a Cuban bandit who joined the Cuban Liberation Army during the War of Cuban Independence.

Venadero" ("The Deer Hunter"). He was a deer hunter, but was also a bandit. He ended up dead inside a well. The authorities killed him and threw his body down the well.

RICARDO COBIÁN: A few leagues from Minas, there was a place called Maldevilla. It was famous for its many bandits who would come around and infiltrate the area through the Artesano Social Club fields. I can't remember the name of one of them, but the Rural Guard captured him, and began striking him with the flat of the blade of the machete all the way down to jail.

FELIPE ROLOFF: I remember that around our area there was a group of peasants who were called "Los Gallos" ("The Gamecocks") and whenever they went there was a gunfight just like the Wild West. They were troublesome because they were bandits during Machado's dictatorship. They caused lots of problems around Morón. The Rural Guard was after them, but they knew the area quite well and knew where to hide.

    I remember one time when I was in charge of the dairy on our farm, I got up at around two in the morning to start milking the cows with the farmhands. As I started brewing coffee, and heard a bunch of shots at a long-distance –one can hear shots in the countryside even from a long distance away– and I later learned that they tried to rob a neighbor of ours named Francisco Hernández, whom we called "Panchito." They tried to rob him at his dairy farm, but Panchito had a shootout with them and killed one of them.

    "Los Gallos," about two months later, returned to rob him and this time they killed "Panchito." The Rural Guard mounted an all-out offensive against them and killed them all. Because of them, I normally used a gun when I got up to milk the cows. It was usual to have a gun around one's waist at the farm.

SECOND PART

CUBA AND ITS HISTORY

THE WAR OF INDEPENDENCE

HORTENSIA LÓPEZ: During the War of Independence, we spent some scary moments because there were many battles between the Spanish and the *Mambises*. The Spanish troops would come from Havana and were quartered at El Caney's Garrison. Since my father was Spanish, the regiment's doctor would stay at our home. Also, once in a while, a Spanish lieutenant or another Spanish officer would stay at my home.

After spending a couple of nights at El Caney, the troops would leave to fight the *Mambises*. Before their departure one would see the Spanish soldiers singing army songs and "La Pilarica." (the Spanish Army fight song). One would have thought that they were going to beat the hell out of the *Mambises* because of their bravado and because they were well equipped. They were riding mules and the mules had huge mulepacks containing food, weapons and ammunition.

The soldiers would spend a week around the backwoods and when they returned to town it was very sad seeing them. Those who had left singing and bragging were now dead. The survivors would bring the wounded in those mulepacks and place them in different homes' porches, so that the doctor could treat them.

One could hear some of them moaning and some of them screaming things like "I'm in pain!" "Mother, please, help me!" "Oh, my God, this is terrible!" One could hear this or that, and it was sad, really, really sad. The majority of the soldiers were less than 18 years old who were sent to fight. Sure, they had rifles, but the *Mambises* fought with machetes which caused lots of casualties among the Spanish. Many of them returned badly wounded, while others died in battles and along the way.

I remember that there were many combats around where I lived. The biggest combat occurred when Maceo was around the area. My father would give us binoculars and we could see people moving from one end to the other. Every night there was a firefight because the *Mambises* would come to town looking for food.

I remember that some Spanish in town had a store named "La Tienda Larga" ("The Long Store,") because it was a whole block long. They had a big mouth, were very boisterous, very cocky and they would make comments around the park making fun of the *Mambises* and ridiculing them. One night, the *Mambises* came into town and set the store on fire. If it weren't for my father and a few others, the homes opposite from that store would have caught on fire.

These people in that store got in trouble with the *Mambises* because of their big mouth. They were asking for it, and they got it. My father, on the contrary, didn't have any problems. Although he was Spanish, he protected many Cubans who went out to join the *Mambises*. At one critical moment in the war, a man named Antonio Quintana, nicknamed "Lao," left the small grocery store he owned and told my father: "Don Pancho, you are the only person I'm telling what I'm going to do. I'm going to join the *Mambises*. I leave my family under your care. I know that you will take care of them and they will not go hungry." So, that's the way it happened. Here was a Cuban with strong convictions, leaving his family with a Spanish to take care of them.

I remember that when the *Mambises* came into town to buy food for their comrades one day, they went to my father's store. They paid my father for bread, but they hurriedly left without taking the bread along, because a Spanish patrol was arriving. Later, when the patrol left, my father took a basketful of bread and headed to the river bank where there was a Spanish fort nearby. He then put the basket on his head, crossed the river and put it on the opposite side of where the *Mambises* were. He was never out to hurt them and everyone loved him.

RODOLFO SOTOLONGO: I wasn't born during the Cuban War of Independence, but my father used to tell me stories, because he fought in that war. My father named me Rodolfo in honor of Rodolfo de los Reyes Gavilán, a *Mambí* friend of his, who died in the war.

My father once told me that when the *Mambises* invaded western Cuba, they had to pass through the plains near Colón. Those plains were very dangerous because there was no cover there, no hills, and nowhere to hide. Besides that, there was Spanish General Martínez Campos[104], camped near Colón with a huge force. Additionally, there was a Spanish fort at the "Antilla"[105] farm, protecting the area.

One day, the *Mambises* decided to attack the fort, but just as they were about to capture it, Spanish reinforcements arrived and the Cubans decided to retreat because their plan wasn't really to take the fort, but rather to hold the Spanish at bay while the other *Mambises* tried crossing the plains.

While the *Mambises* were cautiously crossing the plains, suddenly, a black man from Oriente Province, drew his machete and a few of the *Mambises* charged the Spanish column's vanguard and kept them at bay. They obviously were killed because it was a small group against the Spanish column of 500 to 600 men. They knew they were going to die but offered their lives so that their countrymen could meet their objective. My father, along with some of the veterans who came to our farm, would sit to chat about the war. Some of them had been on the cavalry, so they would talk about their favorite weapon, the machete. The Spanish were terrified of the *Mambí* cavalry because they were very daring, and used the machete. The Spanish, for example, would charge with bayonets drawn, but, despite those charges, the *Mambí* cavalry would

---

[104] Arsenio Martínez Campos (1831-1900). Captain-General of Cuba from 1876 until 1879 and from 1895 until 1896. Although Martínez Campos put an end to the Ten Years' War, he failed to crush the Cuban War of Independence. Born in Segovia, Spain, on December 14, 1831, he died in Zarauz, Spain, on September 23, 1900.

[105] The Battle of Antilla took place on December 2, 1895. The Cuban patriots achieved an important victory in defeating a Spanish column under General García Navarro.

attack them with their famous machete charge and the Spanish would disband in disarray. One thing must be made perfectly clear, the Spanish were not cowards. The Spanish soldier has always been a brave soldier and in Cuba, the Spanish fought valiantly. Even though they were fighting for an unjust cause, they fought bravely.

CEREFINO GARCÍA: Of course, I didn't fight in the War of Independence, because I didn't arrive in Cuba until 1915, but I remember that one of our clients would tell me stories about the war and he would say: "My parents used to take me where the Spanish soldiers were camping out and they would give us food. In fact, the soldiers said that while they were there, no one was going to go hungry. They didn't throw away any food. They were so good to us that we ate what they ate."

MANUEL GARCÍA IGLESIAS: During the War of Independence, my grandfather, a Spanish, was on board a train loaded with Spanish troops from Sagua to Santa Clara. The *Mambises* attacked the train, inflicting several casualties on the Spanish and the troops wouldn't do anything because the *Mambises* simply vanished. I believe they were under General Robau's[106] command, who was operating around the area.

In the Sagua area, there was also a captain named Sánchez Gorro, known as "El Pelón" ("The Bald One"). The Spanish killed him. They picked up his body, took it to a place near the river and exposed it to the whole town as a warning of what could happen to them.

My father was about to join *the Mambises* with a group of friends who were about 16 years old. However, their elders grabbed them and said: "Don't go, because if they capture you,

---

[106] José Luis Robau (1870-1909). General of the Cuban Liberation Army during the Cuban War of Independence and Governor of Las Villas Province from 1908 until 1909. He was born in Sagua la Grande, on October 3, 1870, and died in said city, on December 12, 1909.

they will send you to the firing squad." That was true, as everyone captured by the Spanish, had to face a firing squad in a place at the back of Sagua's jail. Later, during the Cuban Republic, an obelisk was built to commemorate those shot by the Spanish.

That war cost a lot of blood and a lot of lives. Then, the Americans entered the war. They got into the war when the *Maine*[107] exploded in Havana Harbor. I have my theory about the incident and I believe that the explosion was caused by the Americans themselves. Neither the Cubans nor the Spanish were in possession of any artifact capable of blowing up a battleship. Besides, it wasn't in the Spanish's best interest to do such a thing. They weren't that stupid to do that.

MARIO VEGA: There wasn't any need for the Americans to have gotten involved in that war because the Cubans had practically won the war. However, the Americans, since the times of Jefferson's administration[108], had an interest in Cuba, so, they simply stuck their nose in that war. I don't know who blew up the *Maine*, because that's a very delicate matter, but I don't believe the Spanish did it.

ANA AURORA RECIO: My father was in Camagüey and my mother found out that he, along with the Marquis of Santa Lucía and two or three more individuals were plotting against the Spanish at a house in Hospital Street, owned by a black woman. It just happened that one of our servants lived near that house and one

---

[107] The *Maine* was not a battleship but rather a cruiser. The 6682 ton *Maine* arrived in Havana on January 24, 1898, with orders to protect American residents in Cuba. On the evening of February 15, 1898, a mysterious explosion rocked the *Maine*, killing 262 crew members. The American Investigating Commission concluded that the explosion was caused by a mine, blaming the Spanish for setting it off. However, recent research has concluded that the explosion was an internal one.

[108] In 1808, President Jefferson sent General James Wilkinson to negotiate with the Marquis of Someruelos, Captain-General of Cuba, the possible purchase of the island by the United States. Spanish officials rejected the offer.

165

day she asked my mother: "Doña Angela, don't you know that about half a block from where I live there are people plotting against the Spanish and that Don Lope and the Marquis go there a lot?"

One evening, my mother put on her shawl, went with the servant to that area, and saw my father entering the house. When my father returned home about one thirty in the morning, she was waiting for him, and told him: "I know you are going to a house to plot against the Spanish because Juana told me so." He answered: "Yes, because the Fatherland is above everything else and I cannot allow my children to live or be born in this kind of slavery that we are currently experiencing." My mother, then, replied: "Well, if you think that what you're doing is in Cuba's best interests, you are doing the right thing." He kept on plotting until one day, he, along with the Marquis and 12 others left for the countryside which was patriot-controlled territory.[109]

About a year and a half after their departure, the Spanish arrested my mother and took her to Camagüey's jail. She was there for a month and a half and then, the Spanish took her to Havana's jail. They informed her that they were going to take her to Chafarinas[110], but, since my mother was an American citizen, she got in touch with the American Consul[111]. He, in turn, forged her documents and her name appeared as Eva Adams. It took a bit of time to do this thing, but the American Consul was able to get her and a few other women out of jail.

When she got out of jail, she sat on a bench wondering what she was going to do because she didn't know where to go.

---

[109] The departure took place on June 12, 1895.

[110] Group of islands near Morocco's northern coast where Cuban patriots or those suspected of aiding them were deported.

[111] Fitzhugh Lee (1835-1905). American Consul in Havana and nephew of Confederate General Robert E Lee. He was also a General during the American Civil War. He was born in Clermont, Virginia, on November 19, 1835 and died in Washington DC, on April 18, 1905. Known as a Cuban Independence sympathizer, many streets in Cuba bear his name.

Somehow, one of my father's friends found out from the Bishop of Havana about her situation and arranged for her to have an audience with Governor Palmerola[112]. She explained her case to him and told him that the reason she had been jailed was because of her husband's activities. She also told him that her children were in Camagüey and that they needed her. Furthermore, she asked Palmerola for permission to return to Camagüey. He, in turn, granted her request and she returned to Camagüey.

Upon returning to Camagüey, the Camagüey Spanish Governor began to pester her, and the Spanish even threatened to tie my ten-year-old brother to the railroad tracks so that the train would run him over. However, some of my father's Spanish friends came to see her and told her: "Angela, they are going to arrest you again." She replied: "I guess I better leave for the countryside to be with Lope."

My mother wrote to my father, informing him about her plans. A few days later, she got a letter from him stating the following: "I'm trying to bribe the Spanish sentries guarding the Camagüey exit road. I will inform you if I'm successful so that you can leave and join me." Finally, one day, my father was successful in bribing the sentries and one day, right at dawn, she left with her six children and the servant.

My mother used to tell me that life in patriot-held territory was hard. She lived in a palm thatched little hut that my father ordered to be made for her. It was so well hidden in that wilderness that my mother could hear the Spanish soldiers' conversation while they were bathing in the river. In the evenings, the servant had to spend about four hours holding a candle to make sure that no snake entered the hut and wrapped itself around one of my brothers' neck. After those four hours, the servant would go to sleep and my mother would replace her all through the night.

---

[112] Don Ignacio Martínez de Despujol y Chávez, Marquis of Palmerola (1859-1937). Civil Governor of Havana in 1897. He was born in Pamplona, Spain, in 1859, and died in said city in 1937.

It was a very difficult life with six children, actually, seven, because one of my sisters was born there in 1898. One of the big problems was the lack of medicine. In 1898, the *Mambises* had two doctors there, Dr. Clark and Dr. Ramón Silva who was a major in the *Mambí* Army. There was also my uncle, but the problem was the lack of medicines. They had to cure the sick with herbal and home remedies. Once in a while, they would get quinine smuggled from Nuevitas, but there was nothing, absolutely nothing.

CELESTINO SUÁREZ: My father was a Spanish volunteer and one day all of the volunteers were called up to reinforce the Jagua Castle Fortress. This was done because the Spanish were hoping for Admiral Cervera[113] to run through the American naval blockade of Santiago de Cuba, set course towards Cienfuegos, replenish his fleet and fight the Americans there under the castle's protection. The castle had long range guns so it was additional protection for his ships.

My father would tell me that while the volunteers were marching towards the castle they would yell out loud: "They have *cañones (cannons),* but we have *cojones* (balls). The problem was that Cervera couldn't run through the blockade because the Americans had much better ships and he was outgunned. Cervera, though, was brave. The man had balls because he knew he was going to lose, but he had to defend the Spanish honor. He lost, but he defended the Spanish honor very well.

FELIPE ROLOFF: When the war of Cuban Independence was going on, my grandfather, General Roloff arrived at Tunas de Za-

---

[113] Don Pascual Cervera y Topete (1839-1909). Commander of the Spanish fleet that faced the American fleet at the Santiago de Cuba Bay Battle on July 3, 1898. After his defeat, he was court-martialed, but acquitted. He was born in Medina Sidonia Spain, on February 18, 1839, and died at Puerto Real, Spain, on April 3, 1909.

za[114] and a few days later, my father joined him. However, it was customary among *Mambises* not to have their sons or relatives under their direct command. This was done to avoid charges of favoritism and have no problems.

My grandfather, then sent him to General Carrillo[115], who was his godfather, but Carrillo sent him on a mission to Oriente Province. In that province, José Maceo[116] was his commander. My father used to say that he had a tough time in that province, because the terrain was unfriendly with lots of thick brush and no resources. As a result, there was a lack of food and they were very hungry. There were lots of birds and rabbits, but soldiers were under strict orders not to shoot them because there was a lack of ammunition. José Maceo wouldn't allow his soldiers to shoot those creatures and if any of his soldiers disobeyed him, he would hit them with the flat of the blade of the machete.

José Maceo "was a tough guy and whenever he lifted his machete up in the air and said "Charge!" people had to follow him because, otherwise, he would hit them with the flat of the blade of the machete. He was an uneducated black man, but very brave. He didn't care if there were 300 or 400 Spanish soldiers confronting him and he only had 100 men. No, sir, when José Maceo said: "Let's go!," everyone had to fight, even the sick had to fight. My father, for example, even though he was General Roloff's son, had to fight, even when he was sick. One time he contracted measles.

---

[114] General Roloff's expedition was the largest ever brought to Cuba during the War of Independence. It was financed by Cuban expatriates living in Key West and Tampa. The expedition arrived at Tunas de Zaza, Las Villas Province, on June 24, 1895.

[115] Francisco Carrillo y Morales (1851-1928). General of the Cuban War of Independence. During the Cuban Republic, he was Governor of Las Villas Province from 1912 until 1920. He was born in Remedios, on October 4, 1851, and died in Havana on May 1, 1928.

[116] José Maceo y Grajales (1841-1896). General of the Cuban War of Independence and Antonio Maceo's brother. He was famous for his bravery in the battlefield. He was born in La Delicia, Oriente Province, on February 2, 1849, and died at the La Loma de Gato Battle, on July 5, 1896.

He was there in Oriente with José Maceo, and he went to battle. He cured himself with sour oranges.

HORTENSIA LÓPEZ: We were there when the Americans started their blockade of Santiago de Cuba and when they landed at Siboney[117]. There, in Santiago, Cervera's fleet was bottled up. It wasn't really a fleet, but rather four or five dilapidated boats. People would make fun of them and even composed a few verses that went like this:

> Cervera has arrived here
> No one should fear
> His ships are made out of tin
> And Admiral Sansón[118] awaits him
> Cervera's cannons just clink
> And his ships are going to sink.

Well, the news that the Americans were going to bomb in Santiago spread like wildfire, so we decided to return to El Caney,[119] because our home over there was big and had huge thick walls. It was a well-protected home. Just as we were about to leave, a man came by and told my father: "It appears that the shelling is not going to happen in a matter of hours. It's going to take some time, so you still have time to take some provisions with you." So, we got out a cracker barrel, chickpeas and rice and we transported them on mules to El Caney.

---

[117] American troops landed at Daiquirí, Oriente Province, on June 22, 1896, and reached Siboney, on June 24, 1898.

[118] Cuban nickname for American Admiral William T Sampson, Commander of the American fleet during the Spanish-American War. Ironically, Admiral Sampson was not at the Santiago de Cuba Bay Battle. He was conducting a meeting with General Shafter, Commander of the American Expeditionary Force. Commodore William Scott Schley, commanded the American fleet at said battle.

[119] Since El Caney had been captured by American and Cuban troops on July 1, 1898, Spanish authorities after a series of negotiations with General Shafter, authorized noncombatants to leave Santiago.

I remember the trip being very hard. My mother was riding on a mule holding my younger brother in her arms and right in the middle of the trip she asked: "Where is my father?" Someone replied: "He's coming in a little while, he's coming." Actually, my grandfather wasn't coming. He didn't want to leave his home in Santiago because he had hidden my father's money under the second bedroom's floor. He remained there in Santiago, guarding that money.

When we reached El Caney, many people came to our home seeking refuge, knowing that we had food. People hardly had anything to eat. They were eating boiled mangoes and escarole. We had food, except for sugar. My father was able to slaughter a calf and distributed the meat among the refugees we had at home.

When the situation calmed down, many returned to Santiago, but we decided to stay at El Caney, and one of my godmother's siblings went to get my grandfather. He was fine because the neighbors fed him and took care of him. Everyone wanted to go to Santiago to see how their properties were doing. They were really worried because they thought their homes had been sacked. There was some looting, but everything was fine.

In Santiago, Our Lady of Mount Carmel Church was packed with people who came to give thanks to Our Lady because Santiago had not been shelled. Over there, near our home in El Caney, there was "El Viso"[120] ("The Vantage Point"), a Spanish fort, and another fort called "El Aceitero"[121]. Around those two

---

[120] One of the many fortifications in the defensive line to protect Santiago de Cuba. In said fort, Spanish General Joaquín Vara del Rey with 576 soldiers held at bay over 6000 American soldiers and over 3000 Cuban soldiers, until running out of ammunition. Vara del Rey died, hit by friendly fire while retreating "El Viso."

[121] Probably referring to the Battle of "El Caldero" (Kettle Hill). Although Colonel Theodore Roosevelt and his Rough Riders have been credited with being the heroes of San Juan Hill, the real heroes were the Ninth and Tenth Regiment soldiers composed of black soldiers known as "The Buffalo Soldiers."

forts, there were serious battles. I didn't witness them because we were in Santiago and they took place before we returned to El Caney. I think that near "El Viso" the Spanish surrendered to the Americans. The ceremony took place under a tree which is called "El Arbol de la Paz."[122] ("The Peace Tree"), but I'm not sure.

---

[122] After a 13 day siege, following the Spanish fleet defeat, Spanish General Francisco Escario, representing General José Toral y Velázquez, Governor of Santiago de Cuba, surrendered to Major Generals Joseph Wheeler and William Lawton. The surrender took place under a *ceiba* (Kapok) tree near San Juan Hill. The tree later became known as "El Árbol de la Paz."

CUBAN PATRIOTS

MARÍA ELBA GONZÁLEZ: As for me, the two greatest Cuban patriots are Martí and Maceo. Martí was an intellectual, a man of unparalleled culture who carried the Cuban ideal throughout the continent. I can say this with authority because throughout the world, people talk about Martí. As far as Maceo is concerned, one doesn't hear much about Maceo, because he was a warrior. He didn't have a formal education, but he was the heart and soul of the Cuban Liberation Army.

FÉLIX MEDINILLA: I believe that the greatest Cuban ever was Antonio Maceo. Lieutenant General Antonio Maceo had six stars, three on each shoulder. Nobody else had as many stars[123]. Maceo was so brave that even the Spanish Queen sent a letter to the Spanish generals, stating the following: "If you capture Maceo, bring him here, because I want to meet him."[124] Maceo, and not Estrada Palma, was the one who had to be the first president of Cuba,[125] because there was an agreement that whomever crossed the Morón *Trocha*[126] first, would be the first Cuban president and Maceo was the first to cross it.

---

[123] The assertion is erroneous, since Maximo Gómez's rank was that of Generalissimo, a higher rank than Maceo's rank.

[124] One of the many myths surrounding the figure of Antonio Maceo.

[125] According to historical sources, no agreement existed between the leaders of the Cuban Liberation Army regarding the crossing of the *Trocha* in the Cuban presidency.

[126] The *Trocha* from Júcaro to Morón in Camagüey Province was a Spanish fortification system. It was 17 leagues in length, containing 33 forts. Around 7000 Spanish soldiers were stationed along this line. General Valmaseda built it during the Ten Years' War. On November 29, 1895 General Maceo crossed it without a single casualty.

LORENZO ZEQUEIRA: Undoubtedly, the two greatest Cuban patriots are José Martí and Antonio Maceo. These two figures inspired many patriotic poems and songs. I remember one - maybe I'll miss a line or two - but it went like this:

> In two different regions
> Two different men were born[127]
> And their ideal was never torn
> The two different men had one common goal
> And Cuban independence was that goal
> In two different regions
> The two different men would fall[128]
> And in Cuban history
> Their memory stands tall.

CELESTINO SUÁREZ: Martí was the Cuban patriot per excellence. However, the sad story is that the eulogy had to be delivered by one of his enemies. When Martí fell in Dos Ríos, the Cuban patriots tried to retrieve his body, but the Spanish had already retrieved it. So, over there, it just happened that there was a Spanish soldier who had known Martí in New York,[129] and he was part of the column that killed Martí. He identified Martí immediately and the body was taken to Santiago de Cuba. When the column reached Santiago, many people came to look at the body. When the time came to bury him in the cemetery, General Sandoval,[130]

---

[127] Martí and Maceo were different in the sense that Martí was white and born in Havana and Maceo was a mulatto born in Oriente Province. Additionally, Martí was a man of letters while Maceo was a military man.

[128] Martí fell in Dos Ríos, in the eastern Province of Oriente, while Maceo fell at San Pedro, between the western Provinces of Havana and Pinar del Río.

[129] Antonio Oliva who was the Spanish column's guide was the one who shot Martí. Captain Enrique Satué Carbonell; who indeed had known Martí in New York, was the one who identified Martí's body.

[130] Colonel José Ximénez de Sandoval y Belange commanded the Spanish column which killed José Martí in Dos Ríos. He was later promoted to general. A native of Málaga, Spain, he died in 1924.

the column's Spanish commander, asked the Cubans at the cemetery if there was a relative, or a good friend, or anyone there who wanted to deliver the eulogy. However, there was absolute silence.

After a few minutes and upon seeing that no one was stepping forward, Sandoval stood erect, and he, himself, delivered the eulogy. The Spanish commander delivered a hell of a eulogy, saying that Martí was a true hero. The irony is that Martí's eulogy had to be delivered by a Spanish, one of Martí's enemies. Can you imagine that? Can one imagine that no Cuban stepped forward to say something about Cuba's greatest hero? Can you imagine that it had to be the Spanish commander, his enemy, the one who delivered the eulogy? Damn it! I know the story well because one of my father's friends who was there told him. Besides, later on, I read something about it. I don't know where because that was a long time ago.

MARIO VEGA: I believe that the greatest Cuban patriots are Carlos Manuel de Céspedes, "The Father of the Country"; José Martí," the Apostle of the Americas"; and Antonio Maceo y Grajales, "The Bronze Titan," symbol of the black man's dignity. Regarding Maceo, I can't believe that a man of Maceo's military stature who always surrounded himself with brave men, could have been killed while resting on a hammock without firing a single shot. It would be presumptuous of me to say what happened because I wasn't there, but I know about Maceo, and I know he was a fighter.

I have my theory about Maceo's death. A man like Maceo who crossed the *Trocha*[131] couldn't have been killed so easily. I think he was killed because he was going to be the first black president of Cuba and many didn't want to see a black president. Unfortunately, in this world, there are many good-for-nothing traitors. The other motive for Maceo's death is that he was a very strong

---

[131] Antonio Maceo crossed two *Trochas,* the already mentioned *Trocha* from Júcaro to Morón and the *Trocha* from Mariel, Havana Province, to Majana, Pinar del Río Province. Maceo crossed this *trocha,* defended by 12,000 Spanish soldiers in August, 1896.

man; a man of character and integrity, and that wasn't in the best interests of certain foreign powers. One must remember Maceo's saying: "Freedom is neither asked, nor begged, it's achieved with the machete's sharp edge." That saying, that mantra was too strong for those "foreign interests" and the evil Cubans who only thought about money.[132]

ENRIQUE CASERO: Cuba has great patriots. However, there have been some that have been forgotten like General Francisco Vicente Aguilera.[133] That man not only had character, but he gave everything he had for Cuba's freedom. He was very rich and I've seen his property deeds somewhere. However, that man only cared about Cuba's freedom.

As far as Carlos Manuel de Céspedes is concerned, it suffices to say that he freed his slaves, and got rid of his sugar mill and went to the hill to fight the Spanish. When the Spanish took his son hostage and informed him that they were going to kill him if he didn't surrender, Céspedes told them to go ahead; he wasn't going to surrender because Cuba's freedom was first[134]. Since the Spanish were stronger, they encircled him, but he wouldn't surrender, and rather than being captured, he committed suicide. Damn it! That's really being a true patriot!

---

[132] There are several versions regarding Maceo's death. Among them, is that of Ramón Vasconcelos, a black Cuban politician who attributed Maceo's death to Cubans. The most authoritarian version regarding Maceo's death is that of José Miró Argenter, Maceo's Chief of Staff and biographer. He attests that the Spanish surprised Maceo while resting in his hammock. Maceo counterattacked with his traditional machete charge. Due to terrain difficulties, the counterattack failed and Maceo was mortally wounded. In addition to Maceo, 12 of his men perished, among them "Panchito" Gómez Toro, Máximo Gómez's son.

[133] Francisco Vicente Aguilera (1821-1871). Major General and Vice President of the Republic in Arms, during the Ten Years' War. Born in Bayamo, on June 23, 1821, he died in New York City, on February 22, 1871.

[134] Spanish authorities took Carlos Manuel de Céspedes' second son, Oscar, hostage and offered Céspedes to respect Oscar's life in exchange for Céspedes resignation as President of the Republic in Arms. When Céspedes refused, Oscar was shot by a Spanish firing squad

FELIPE ROLOFF: My grandfather wasn't only a general in the Cuban War of Independence, but he already had been a general in the Ten Years' War. After the American Civil War, he went to Caribarién, a port in Las Villas Province, to work for an American sugar company. He was a naturalized American citizen and had been a captain for the north in that war. My grandfather was good friends with Emilio Núñez Rodríguez,[135] Serafín Sánchez,[136] and Francisco "Pancho" Carrillo. When the Céspedes and Agramonte uprisings took place in 1868, my grandfather and his friends rebelled against the Spanish in Las Villas. They took off for the countryside and fought the Spanish for almost 10 years until the Pacto del Zanjón,[137] which ended the war.

After the pact, my grandfather left for Honduras. He was well off there, because he, Don Tómas Estrada Palma, Rius Rivera and the poet Joaquín Palma[138] were all married to President Guardiola's[139] daughters. They were all economically in good shape, until Martí called on them to fight for Cuba's freedom. All of them went to fight, except Palma, who was a civilian. My grandfather left for the United States and was in charge of coordinating the pa-

---

[135] Emilio Núñez Rodríguez (1856-1922). General in the Ten Years' War of Cuban Independence. He was Governor of Havana from 1901 until 1908. Born in Sagua la Grande, on December 22, 1855, he died in Havana, on March 5, 1922.

[136] Serafín Sánchez Valdivia (1846-1896). General in the Ten Years' War and the War of Cuban Independence. Born in Sancti Spíritus on July 2, 1846, he died at the Pasos de Las Damas Battle, on November 18, 1896.

[137] Pact signed on February 10, 1878 between the Ten Years' War Cuban leaders and General Arsenio Martínez Campos, Spanish Captain-General of Cuba. Despite protests from Antonio Maceo and other leaders, the pact ended the Ten Years' War.

[138] José Joaquín Palma (1844-1911). The last of the Romantic Cuban poets and composer of the Guatemalan national anthem. Born in Bayamo, on September 11, 1844, he died in Guatemala City, on August 2, 1911.

[139] José Santos Guardiola (1816-1862). Honduran president from 1856 until 1862. Known for his democratic reforms, he was assassinated while still in office. Born in Tegucigalpa, Honduras, on November 1, 1816, he died in Camayagua, Honduras, on January 11, 1862.

triots' military expeditions to Cuba. According to El Cacahual[140] Monument's plaque, my grandfather was the general who brought the most expeditions to Cuba. After his last expedition, he was named Chief of Military Operations in Las Villas and he ended up as Inspector General of the Cuban Liberation Army.

There's an event that happened that is not in the history books and that's the fact that he was court-martialed. It happened that he was camped out with his men near Yaguajay in Las Villas. Apparently, the sentinels got careless, the Spanish caught them off guard, attacked furiously, and all hell broke loose. My grandfather got on a horse, but the horse was tied to a post and he couldn't leave. He then saw a black *Mambí* running and said to him: "Hey! Cut this rope off, and I'll make you a sergeant!" However, the guy didn't, he kept on running because there were bullets flying everywhere. So, my grandfather had no other alternative than to get his gun and shoot the rope. Because he was a great marksman, the bullet hit the rope and he was able to escape.

After the surprise attack, he was court-martialed and condemned to death. Generalissimo Máximo Gómez, the Supreme Commander, had to confirm the death penalty. Gómez arrived at the site and addressed my grandfather: "General Roloff, because of your carelessness we lost several men and you deserve the death penalty. However, Cuba needs you. Therefore, I commute your sentence, so that you can continue fighting for Cuba. Let's continue fighting for Cuba until independence is achieved."

My grandfather was a true patriot and a true veteran. There were many who claimed to be veterans, but they weren't veterans, they never fought. All they did was to bring quinine to the *Mambises*. They would spend a day with them and return to town. These people never fought; therefore, they weren't veterans. All of the veterans' names that fought for Cuba are recorded in my grandfather's book *El Índice del Ejército Libertador (Index of the*

---

[140] Small hill in Havana Province. The monument contains Antonio Maceo's remains.

Liberation Army). If a name doesn't appear in that book, then, the person claiming to be a veteran, wasn't a veteran.

VICTOR VEGA CEBALLOS: My two favorite Cuban patriots are both Camagüeyans and both were cousins: Gaspar Betancourt Cisneros,[141] and Salvador Cisneros Betancourt. Gaspar Betancourt Cisneros was an extraordinary human being. He fought against ignorance and injustices. He also fought against a firmly entrenched society full of prejudices and unprogressives. He fought for change.

He, for example, was responsible for bringing the railroad to Camagüey, making it the second Cuban city to have a railroad. At that time, people were saying that the railroad was going to end the Camagüeyan way of life and that evil people were going to come to Camagüey by train. They were also saying that trains were prone to accidents and many people were going to be killed. However, "El Lugareño" ("The Villager"), as he was called, brought the railroad from Camagüey to Nuevitas. Sadly, he lost his entire fortune in bringing the railroad.

"El Lugareño" was a great conspirator against the Spanish domination. At first he was in favor of the American annexation of Cuba because he thought that Cuban independence was impossible, but later on in life, he became an independentist. He was so well respected and beloved that when he died in Havana, all the people in that city mourned him. His body was transported by sea to Nuevitas and from there was taken to Camagüey where he was buried with honors.

Gaspar Betancourt Cisneros's cousin, Salvador Cisneros Betancourt, Marquis of Santa Lucía, was also a great patriot who gave everything for Cuba's freedom. The Marquis was a true democrat who didn't believe in nobility titles and all of that nonsense. He was simply a pragmatic individual. The title of Marquis of San-

---

[141] Gaspar Betancourt Cisneros (1803-1866). Cuban writer and patriot. Born in Camagüey, on April 29, 1803, he died in Havana, on December 7, 1866.

ta Lucía, was the only nobility title allowed in Camagüey under the Cuban Republic. There's not a single individual in Camagüey who doesn't know who the Marquis of Santa Lucía was. The Marquis used to make fun of nobility titles by referring to them as "aliases" and "nicknames." The Marquis of Santa Lucía, by the way, was the only Cuban legislator that when Estenoz and Ivonet[142] wanted to form a black political party, he said: "Why not?" "They are entitled to do so. They have the right to establish it because they are Cubans too."

ANA AURORA RECIO: My father, Lope Recio y Loynaz even became a Major General in the *Mambí* Army. As soon as he left to fight the Spanish, they named him major and quickly, he rose through the ranks because of his bravery. At one point he commanded 5000 *Mambises*. He lost five horses during the war and five times his aides had to pick him up from where he had fallen. However, the minute he fell, the minute he continued fighting. He fought the Spanish with his machete in hand.

They said my father was something else handling a machete and that the Spanish were terrified of my father's cavalry. Once Cuba became independent and disagreements and fights broke out among Cubans, my father resigned his political post and told my mother: "I'm returning to my farm; I can't stand fights among brothers."

FELIPE ROLOFF: The most brilliant strategist in the Cuban War of Independence was Generalissimo Máximo Gómez. He was a true soldier. He had been trained in Santo Domingo and I think he rose to the rank of captain there. He fought in the Ten Years' War and later, in the War of Independence, he was the invasion's plan-

---

[142] Evaristo Estenoz and Pedro Ivonet were the cofounders of the Independent Colored Party in 1908, and leaders of the ill-fated commonly called "The Little Race War of 1912." The Cuban Senate's vote as to the party's legality was three in favor and 12 opposed. Judging from the vote results, the Marquis de Santa Lucía was not the only legislator in favor.

ner. The invasion was something else because the *Mambises* had to march from East to West and the Spanish had numerous fortifications along the way.

The Generalissimo was a great patriot. Besides being a brave man, he was a great diplomat with a great sense of humor. For example, when Martí and Maceo met at "La Mejorana"[143] to plan the invasion and discuss Cuba's future, there were apparently disagreements between the two of them, but Máximo Gómez, with his diplomatic skills, brought them together.

As far as his sense of humor is concerned, my father who ended up on his staff told me an anecdote. He said that when Máximo Gómez reached Havana, everyone came out to welcome him and told him how hard they fought for Cuba's freedom. He then turned to one of his aides and said: "Hell, if I just had all of these people here during the war, I would had beaten the Spanish by just swatting my hat."

The man was a true human being and when they came to offer him the Cuban presidency, he simply told them: "Men of war, for war, men of peace, for peace." He rejected the Cuban presidency because he knew his limitations. I remember a poem about Máximo Gómez that went like this:

> A horse he could ride
> And was brave in the fight
> He was a man of reason
> Who hated treason
> The machete he used to wield
> Made the Spanish run in the field
> For Cuba he fought
> And freedom he brought.

---

[143] Farm in Oriente Province where a meeting between Martí, Maceo and Gómez took place. There have been numerous speculations as to what transpired at "La Mejorana." Unfortunately, the pages where Martí narrated the event were torn from his diary.

THE AMERICAN OCCUPATION OF CUBA

JOSEFINA PÉREZ: Since I was born in 1891, I still remember the American occupation. I was just a girl and I was visiting the Jagua Castle Fortress when I heard an alarm. What caused the alarm was that a boatload of drunken American soldiers made a sharp turn around Pasacaballos and it capsized. One would see some of them swimming and the other ones reaching shore, looking like a bunch of wet chickens. I can't remember the year, but I remember the time. It was three in the afternoon when it happened.

During the American occupation in Cienfuegos, the soldiers were quartered by the sanatorium and their commander was Major Clark[144]. He lived on Lamar Street between Cristina Street and Prado Street. He lived about three houses from where I lived. He was married and had two children. They all were very kind, but didn't speak a word of Spanish.

FELIPE ROLOFF: Of course, I hadn't been born during the American occupation, but my father told me that there was an American judge in Havana who was very strict and really hit the mule cart drivers very hard. He wanted the Havana Streets to be squeaky clean and didn't want the mules to be shitting on the streets. So, this judge began to impose stiff fines on them. They used to call him Mr. Piche[145], so people started saying: "Mr. Piche is tough,

---

[144] Wallis O'Clark (1854-1914). American Army Major and Governor of Camagüey Province from 1898 until 1899 during the American occupation of Cuba. Born in Chelsea, Massachusetts, in 1854, he died in Boston, on September 14, 1914.

[145] Although the Cubans called him Mr. Piche, he was J.J. Pitcher, an American judge in Havana during the American occupation of Cuba from 1898 until 1902.

Mr. Piche is rough, a $10 fine you are going to get if your mule on the streets does shit."

ANA AURORA RECIO: The American governors during the American occupation of Cuba were John Brooke[146] and Leonard Wood[147]. My father used to say that General Wood was the one who named my father Governor of Camagüey. Wood did whatever my father told him to do because he didn't speak Spanish and my father knew English. Wood trusted my father so much that he used to say: "Whatever General Recio says, I'll do it."

When the American occupation ended, Wood left Cuba, but he kept corresponding with my father. In one of his letters, he wrote my father the following: "General, the day you want to leave for the United States and become an American citizen, all you have to do is to write to me, and I will immediately get you American citizenship. You are a man who honors your country, and I know the type of man you are." According to my father, Wood was a great man and a great governor.

VÍCTOR VEGA CEBALLOS: During the American occupation, they appointed a guy named Mr. Frye[148] in charge of education in Cuba. This man decreed that parents with school age children had

---

[146] John Brooke (1838-1926). American Army General and first Governor of Cuba from January 1, 1899 until December 20, 1899, during the American occupation of Cuba. Born in Pottstown, Pennsylvania, on July 1, 1838, Brooke, the last surviving Union general, died in Philadelphia, on September 5, 1926.

[147] Leonard Wood (1860-1927). American Army General and second Governor of Cuba during the American occupation of Cuba. He was in charge from December 20, 1899 until May 20, 1902. Born in Winchester, New Hampshire, on October 9, 1860, he died in Boston, on August 7, 1927.

[148] Alexis Frey was Professor of Education at the University of Chicago. General Brooke appointed him as Superintendent General of Education in Cuba. Frye was responsible for the establishment of numerous schools in Cuba. However, Governor Wood relieved him of his duties because of differences regarding education in Cuba.

to send them to school, and failure to do so would result in a court trial and fine. A number of parents were sent to court and fined. The parents' reason for not sending their kids to school was that sending them to school meant that they had to give them breakfast and since they were poor, they couldn't afford breakfast. In other words, they couldn't send them on an empty stomach. Additionally, they said that they couldn't send them to school because they couldn't afford shoes. The parents really weren't giving excuses; they were just citing their predicament.

During the beginning of the 20th century, Cuba was a poor country, devastated by war. The Americans were interested in education, but they didn't understand the Cuban reality. They didn't understand the parents' poor economic conditions. Taking into consideration that the situation was really serious, my uncle, Liborio, organized the Masons and both Masons and non-Masons began donating money to two causes: "The School Breakfast," and "The School Shoes." As a result of his efforts, those two problems were solved.

I remember that with the contributions, children were given shoes. Their top was made out of a type of cloth called "Tela de Rusia" ("Russian Cloth"), similar to canvas, and their soles were very thin. Don Cirilo Sarbatela, a mulatto, used to sell those shoes. He would carry a pole on his shoulders with the shoes hanging from each end. Later on, the Cuban government took over the "School Breakfast" entity and incorporated it to the Ministry of Education's budget. Many of the big buildings in Miami were built with the "School Breakfast" budget. Some politicians whose names I don't want to mention, stole the money earmarked in the budget and invested it in Miami a few years ago. If my poor uncle would see what they did with that entity which he created, he would be rolling in his grave.

ESTRADA PALMA'S ARRIVAL AND MAXIMO GÓMEZ'S FUNERAL

CARLOS MONTERO: I remember Estrada Palma's arrival in Havana. I don't know if it was exactly on May 20, 1902, but I remember that he arrived by ship.[149] I remember going to a field near the *malecón*, between the gazebo and the jail. It was a huge field and it was packed with people. Later on, Estrada Palma came to Belén, my school, and decorated me with a medal.

HORTENSIA LÓPEZ: Estrada Palma was inaugurated as president of Cuba on May 20, 1902, but later on, he undertook a trip around the island and went to Santiago. There, in Santiago, they gave him a huge reception. The streets were decorated with Cuban flags and the corner stores had thick ribbons on the top from corner to corner. There were also these baskets hanging from those ribbons and just as Don Tomás was passing under the ribbons, a number of white doves came out of those baskets, flying into the sky.

Don Tomás looked like a venerable old man. He was seated on the back of his open carriage wearing his suit and a top hat. I must point out that the stores from where the doves came out were Spanish-owned and for those Spanish store owners, it was an honor welcoming such a venerable Cuban. Before I got married, Don Tomás lived on 9 Peña Pobre Street. My husband used to see Don Tomás riding in his carriage to leave his children at school.

Another event I witnessed was Máximo Gómez's funeral in June, 1905.[150] I don't remember the exact day, but we were visit-

---

[149] Estrada Palma arrived in Havana on board the steamship *Julia* on May 11, 1902.

[150] Generalissimo Máximo Gómez died on June 17, 1905 and his funeral was on June 18, 1905.

ing in Havana and people were having a festival in the district where we were staying. Suddenly, the police arrived, notifying the people that the festival had to be canceled, because Máximo Gómez had died. At first, people didn't believe the news and wanted to proceed with the festival, but they canceled it.

    The funeral was the next day and my uncle and I went to El Vedado to see the funeral procession. It was so big and unbelievable. He wasn't a Cuban, but he was a great patriot. Cubans loved him and he was very popular. However his popularity might have cost him his life. The political situation in Cuba was bleak with many rivalries. Since he was always seeking peace and unity among Cubans, he went to different provinces, trying to make peace among the rivals. He had a sore on his right hand's palm and from so many handshakes it became infected and the infection caused his death.

THE 1906 "LITTLE WAR"

FELIPE ROLOFF: I know the true story of "La guerrita de 1906" (The 1906 "Little War") because my grandfather was the Treasurer of the Cuban Republic under Don Tomás Estrada Palma. Everything started when Don Tomás decided to go up for reelection and his opponents didn't like that. I don't think it was his ego which prompted him to make that decision. On the contrary, I think he did it out of his sense of duty and in good faith.

Don Tomás wanted to pay off a $35 million debt which Cuba had incurred from the United States at the start of his presidency. Unfortunately, it was impossible to have the $35 million in the treasury. As a matter of fact, my grandfather only had $28 million in the treasury. So, Don Tomás figured that if he stayed on as president, the loan would be paid off during his second term. He just simply wanted Cuba to be debt free. The Americans, on the other hand, didn't want Cuba to pay off the loan because they wanted to economically tie down Cuba, and not paying the debt was the way to do it.

Don Tomás went up for reelection and the State Department engineered an uprising in Cuba. The Americans enticed a bunch of brave but incompetent generals from the War of Independence to stage an uprising under the pretext of "no reelection." So, in 1906, Pino Guerra[151] staged a revolt in Pinar del Río. It was followed by another uprising under Quintín Banderas[152] in Havana

---

[151] Faustino "Pino" Guerra. Colonel in the Cuban Liberation Army who later became a congressman from Pinar del Río Province. During José Miguel Gómez's presidency (1909-1913), he became Cuban Army Chief of Staff.

[152] Quintín Banderas (1837-1906). General in the War of Independence, famous both for his daring and bravery. Born in Santiago de Cuba, on January 1, 1837, he was assassinated in a farm near Arroyo Arenas, Havana Province, on August 22, 1906.

Province. He was an illiterate black general, very brave, but politically incompetent. The Cuban Army captured him and he was hacked to pieces.

Realizing that the situation was getting out of hand, Don Tomás called in his military commanders, informed them that he was not going to continue as president and asked the United States to militarily intervene in Cuba. The United States, seeing a golden opportunity to keep Cuba in debt, decided to intervene.[153]

I know all of this because my father told me that his grandfather had told him the whole story. My grandfather handed the Americans the $28 million, but I don't know what they did with them. I guess they wanted to pay off those who started the revolt, but I think they only gave them a few cents.

RODOLFO SOTOLONGO: I don't remember what triggered "La guerrita," but I do remember it was against Don Tomás. I was nearly five years old, but I recall that we had visitors at the farm and were having a pig roast. We had a black youngster who worked at the farm. He had gone to transfer a horse from the backwoods to pastureland. Apparently, there were some rebels around the area who mistook him for a soldier or an informer and shot him dead. I saw when some of the farmhands brought his slumped body on horseback. We immediately suspended all activities because we were simply devastated. I have never been able to forget that incident. I was nearly 5, and sadly, I still remember it.

JOSEFINA PÉREZ: I remember "La guerrita." It was really the product of the rivalry between José Miguel Gómez's Liberals and Estrada Palma's supporters. In Cienfuegos, in 1905, prior to "La guerrita," the situation had reached a boiling point. There was a

---

[153] There are several versions regarding the 1906 American intervention of Cuba. However, there is historical evidence that the intervention was partially provoked by pro-American annexionists, among them was Frank Steinhart, American Consul in Cuba.

shootout between Illance[154] and Villuendas[155] at the La Suiza Hotel. Villuendas was a Liberal Party Congressman from Cienfuegos. Illance was Cienfuegos's Police Chief and was married to Cuca Valdés.

It seems that Villuendas had come to Cienfuegos to have a political rally and Illance came to the hotel to arrest him under the pretext that there were weapons inVilluendas's room. One of Villuendas's bodyguards upon seeing Illance trying to arrest Villuendas, shot him dead. Illance's men, in turn, shot Villuendas dead and mayhem broke out in Cienfuegos. A doctor who was the Health Department Director in Cienfuegos was also killed. I'm not sure about his last name, but I think it was Figueroa.

I was about 13 or 14 and I remember it was on September 22, 1905. I remember it very well because things got out of hand in Cienfuegos and my aunt and I left for Manzanillo. Life is funny, full of irony. It just happened that there is a park in Cienfuegos named Villuendas Park and this lady, Cuca Valdés, Illance's widow, lived right across from the park.

---

[154] Angel Illance. Colonel in the Cuban Liberation Army and Cienfuegos's Chief of Police during Estrada Palma's administration.

[155] Enrique Villuendas. Colonel in the Cuban Liberation Army and a Liberal Party Congressman from Las Villas Province.

ESTENOZ'S AND IVONET'S "LITTLE RACE WAR"

RODOLFO SOTOLONGO: I remember the 1912 Estenoz's[156] and Ivonet's[157] "Little Race War." They both had been officers in the War of Independence, and in the Cuban Republic they wanted to establish a black political party. However, there was a law whose main proponent was a black senator[158] which prohibited parties based on race, creed or nationality. As a result, Estenoz and Ivonet led an uprising in Oriente Province because they were determined to establish a black party by reason or by force.

At that time, José Miguel[159] was the president and Monteagudo was the Army Chief of Staff. Troops were sent to Oriente and they killed many blacks. Some of the blacks were killed in combat, but it was a grave injustice that the majority of them were killed in cold blood, without having any participation whatsoever

---

[156] Evaristo Estenoz, cofounder of the *Partido Independiente de Color* was the son of a French father and a Cuban mother. He was a lieutenant in the Cuban Liberation Army and an aide to General Quintín Banderas. A fighter for Afro-Cuban rights, he led the uprising in 1912 known as "The Little Race War." On June 27, 1912, the Cuban Army shot him point-blank near Alto Songo, Oriente Province.

[157] Pedro Ivonet Dofourt. Brigadier General in the Cuban Liberation Army. Cofounder of the *Partido Independiente de Color* and one of the leaders of the 1912 "Little Race War." Allegedly of Haitian ancestry, Ivonet was captured near El Caney. On July 18, 1912, mulatto Lieutenant Arsenio Oritz shot him while "trying to escape."

[158] Martín Morúa Delgado (1856-1910). Prominent Afro-Cuban writer and the first black President of the Cuban Senate. He was the principal architect of the Ley Morúa, banning political parties based on color, creed or nationality. He was born in Matanzas, on November 11, 1856 and died in Havana, on April 28, 1910.

[159] José Miguel Gómez (1858-1921). General of the Cuban War of Independence, Leader of the Liberal Party and second president of Cuba (1909-1913). He was born in Sancti Spíritus, in 1858, and died in New York City, in 1921.

in the uprising. People began calling it "La guerrita racista." ("The Little Race War"). Estenoz and Ivonet were also killed in that war.

I remember a rather funny incident that happened during that war. In my hometown, a citizen's militia began patrolling key sectors, especially the town's entry and exit points. While people were strolling in the park during an evening, one of the militiamen, acting as a sentry at a place called "La Loma," right at the town's entrance; heard a noise in the darkness. He yelled: "Halt!" "Halt!" several times and no answer, only the noise. He, then, opened fire and others started shooting.

The shots were heard in the park and women wearing long dresses began running for dear life. It was a stampede and their dresses began to shred as they were running for cover. Some of the ladies sought refuge at nearby houses; others managed to reach their homes exhausted. What really happened that night was a false alarm. The sentry had mistaken a poor cow for a rebel and since the cow couldn't respond, it was shot to pieces.

CARLOS MONTERO: I entered the academy right in 1912 because I always wanted to be where the action was and that "guerrita" prompted me to enter the academy. I had heard that the blacks in Oriente had killed some people and had set a town on fire. However, I didn't go there because the Cuban Army Academy Director, Lezama, did not get involved in politics and just wanted to make professional soldiers out of us.

FELIPE ROLOFF: I didn't witness Estenoz's and Ivonet's "Little Race War," but I can tell about it, based on what people have told me. I believe that Estenoz and Ivonet didn't provoke that uprising. Its author was José Miguel, because he was a racist. Apparently, through some of his contacts, he enticed the blacks to stage an uprising. Those contacts began to spread rumors among the black population in Oriente, regarding unfairness and discrimination in that province. It was a trap. He just needed an excuse to get rid of the blacks. Estenoz and Ivonet took the bait, and the rest is history.

Many blacks were killed in Oriente[160]. There was an army captain, whose name, I think was Cadenas. He took a group of black prisoners and told them: "Stand here, because we have to take your picture." The tripod camera was covered, but when the cover was lifted, it wasn't a camera, but a machine gun. They were massacred. Since many blacks had been killed, a number of politicians went to see José Miguel to protest the atrocities. They went to him and said: "General, those people have been wrongly killed." José Miguel replied: "Yes, they have been wrongly killed, but they are dead all right."

ENRIQUE CASERO: I was just a nine-year-old kid when that war took place, but I saw when they were transporting Ivonet's body to the Moncada Barracks. I'm from Santiago and I saw that. It appears that he was captured alive. I believe that Estenoz committed suicide, but Ivonet was taken prisoner. The army took him to the other side of the bay and one of the officers told him: "Just wait here a bit. A schooner is going to pick you up, and everything is going to be fine." Well, no schooner came and he was murdered there in cold blood.

---

[160] There are many versions regarding the cause of "The Little Race War." One theory is that José Miguel instigated the revolt, only to put it down and ensure his reelection. Another theory blames Steinhart for instigating the revolt to provoke an American intervention leading to the possible annexation of Cuba.

LIBERALS AND CONSERVATIVES

RODOLFO SOTOLONGO: Political campaigns between Liberals[161] and Conservatives[162] were passionate campaigns, especially during José Miguel Gómez's and Mario García Menocal's[163] times. There were many slogans and riddles. I remember one the Conservatives sang:

> On November 1st
> The winner is going to be Menocal
> And the one who doesn't have a horse
> It's going to ride on a Liberal[164].

The Liberals also had their famous son called "La Chambelona" ("The Lollipop") which went like this:

> AE, AE, AE "La *Chambelona*"
> I'm not to blame
> I'm not to blame

I remember that during the elections for Mayor of Havana between Conservative Party candidate Aspiazu,[165] famous for dis-

---

[161] Members of the Partido Liberal, a Cuban political party founded and led by José Miguel Gómez as an opposition party to Estrada Palma's Partido Moderado.

[162] Members of the Conservative Party, a Cuban political party established after Estrada Palma's resignation in 1906. It was established by Liberal Party dissidents and members of the defunct Partido Moderado.

[163] Mario García Menocal y Deop (1866-1941). A graduate of Cornell's University School of Engineering, Menocal was a Major General in the Cuban War of Independence. During the Cuban Republic, he became the leader of the Partido Conservador and third President of Cuba from 1913 until 1921

[164] In Spanish, the word liberal is stressed on the final vowel.

[165] A Havana political boss, famous for the granting of "botellas." He was the Partido Conservador mayoral candidate in the 1916 elections. Despite his widespread granting of *"botellas",* he was defeated.

tributing non-existing government jobs, known as *"botellas"* among his supporters, and Liberal Party candidate Varona,[166] the students had a riddle that went like this:

> Ae, Ae, Ae, "La Chambelona"
> Aspiazu gave me a "botella"
> But I voted for Varona
> Ae, Ae, Ae, "La Chambelona"
> The School of Medicine will go
> And they will all vote
> All the way for Varona.

VÍCTOR VEGA CEBALLOS: In Cuba, there was a deep political rivalry between the Liberals and Conservatives. I can attest to the rivalry because I came from a family whose members were founders and champions of the Liberal Party. As a matter of fact, my father, my uncle, and my brother-in-law gave their lives for the Liberal cause. One of the salient features of this rivalry was its comical side. A few months before scheduled elections, each party would come out singing its "Battle Hymn" which was funny in nature.

In the 1916 presidential elections, the Conservatives came out with its famous "Tumba la Caña," ("Cut the sugar cane stalk") because prior to being president, Menocal had been the Chaparra sugar mill general manager and a long time ago, general managers and sugar mill canefield overseers were referred to as *mayorales*. It went like this:

> Cut out the cane
> And give me no grief
> Here comes Menocal
> Cracking the whip.

---

[166] Manuel Varona Suárez, a famous medical doctor, was one of the Partido Liberal's leaders. He was Mayor of Havana from 1916 until 1920 and later served as Senator of the Cuban Republic.

The Liberals, in turn, took the tune from a popular song called "La Chambelona" and added their own words. One of the refrains went like this:

> Ae, Ae, Ae, "La Chambelona"
> I'm not ashamed
> I'm not to blame
> Ae, Ae, Ae, "La Chambelona"
> The first of November
> Will be a day to be remembered
> The government will be dismembered
> And, their loss they[167] will remember

There were towns in Cuba that were extremely in the hands of the Liberal Party and others where the Conservative Party reigned. For example, the town of Puerto Padre, Oriente Province, was so conservative that even the rocks were conservative. In that town, I helped to increase the Liberal Party membership. However I had lots of Conservative Party friends. Menocal's nephews and I were good friends. They even helped me to enable the Liberals to win in that town. I remember they used to say to me: "We are Víctor Vega's Liberals in this town, but outside this town, we are our uncle's followers."

RICARDO COBIÁN: In my town, the biggest political parties were the Liberal and Conservative parties. There were two big *caciques* (party bosses) who dominated politics in that town: Manolo Quintana, the Liberal Party boss and Eloy García Miranda, the Conservative Party boss. Sometimes, there was tension between the two of them, but at times, they would make peace among themselves.

I remember that one time there was a machete duel between Leoncio, one of García Miranda's brothers and "Manín," Quintana's son. The duel was because of their political rivalry and

---

[167] The Conservatives.

both of them hurt each other. However, when the Rural Guard officers arrived, they both said that nothing had happened. They were both well known in town; no charges were filed.

CARLOS MONTERO: In the Víbora District there was a trolley stop and next to it there was a Banyan tree where both Liberals and Conservatives had their political rallies. One day, I saw a big fight between them. One of the leaders was a peggedleg guy who had been shot there by someone from the other party. His rival from the other party was a midget who had been a pimp. He was a tough little cookie. One day, I saw that midget in a fight where he shot one of his rivals.

MANUEL GARCÍA IGLESIAS: In Sagua, there were two big political parties, the Liberal and the Conservative. Later on, another party, the Popular Party[168] emerged. That party had a small membership and people made fun of it by calling it "El Partido de los Cuatro Gatos" (The Teenie Weenie Party"). Alfredo Zayas was the leader. Later on, he was elected president when the party allied itself with the Conservatives.
I was a Conservative, but it was hard for us to win an election in Sagua, because Sagua was Liberal country. The Liberals used to win most of the times because of their promises to the lower classes. During provincial elections, it was not unusual for party candidates to be kidnapped, so that they would be unable to campaign. The kidnapped candidates were well-treated, and nothing happened to them. However, since they couldn't campaign, it was hard for them to win. Both parties did it, so it was "the same dog with a different collar."

---

[168] The Partido Popular Cubano, was a minor Cuban political party led by Alfredo Zayas. Zayas became President of Cuba (1920-1924), as a result of an alliance between Menocal's Conservative followers and his party. The alliance was known as the Liga Nacional (National League).

THE "CHAMBELONA" UPRISING

VÍCTOR VEGA CEBALLOS: I remember the "Chambelona" uprising as if it happened today. That uprising took place in Camagüey a bit before 10 in the evening when the Camagüey-based Army Regiment under Colonel Enrique Quiñones and his aide, Lieutenant Colonel Eliseo Figueroa, revolted. By the way, Figueroa fought bravely at the Battle of Antón, the only battle won by the rebels.

The uprising was the product of Menocal's reelection. The elections had taken place on November 1, 1916. The Liberals had clearly won the elections, but the Canvassing Board changed the election results and fraudulently, declared Menocal the winner. The Liberals took the case to the Supreme Court which declared José Miguel Gómez the winner. However, Menocal rejected the Supreme Court's decision, and as a result, José Miguel Gómez, the Liberal Party presidential candidate revolted[169].

In Camagüey, for example, the Liberals had won the mayoral elections. In our city, there was numerical parity between Liberals and Conservatives and the mayoral election results were very close. Usually, the winner of those elections would win by no more than 50 votes. I don't know what happened, but apparently, one of the Canvassing Board clerks made a mistake in totaling the results and recorded 47 votes for the Conservatives and 17 votes for the Liberals in a particular area known to be Liberal. The recording should have been the other way around.

The Liberals were confident of their victory, but the Canvassing Board had already declared the Conservative candidate as the winner. Both sides began to hold marches declaring victory. Finally, when the Canvassing Board admitted its error, it was too

---

[169] The uprising happened on February 10, 1917.

late, for the uprising in Camagüey was already taking place. I would say that about half of the city's population joined the uprising.

MARÍA ELBA GONZÁLEZ: The uprising was in 1917. José Miguel Gómez was the winner, but Menocal stole the elections from him. So, José Miguel went to the backwoods to fight. Army commanders Collazo[170] and Consuegra[171] went to Placetas in Las Villas Province and near Placetas at a hill called Caicaje,[172] there was a battle between José Miguel's followers and the Cuban Army.

After he lost the battle, José Miguel fled, but was captured seeking refuge at a lady's home. He was knocking at the door and when the lady came out to open the door, one of her sons who was nearby was hit by a bullet which killed him instantly. José Miguel was captured, but was later freed and died here in the United States. His body was transported to Cuba for burial. It was probably the largest funeral in Cuban history. All of Prado Boulevard was covered with funeral wreaths. The funeral was in 1921.

CARLOS MONTERO: When the "Chambelona" revolt broke out I was a Lieutenant in the First Battalion, Second Company. That revolt was a rather severe one because half of the Cuban Army had sided with the rebels. Each military district had a colonel in charge. Some of the colonels were loyal to the government and others joined the rebels. The whole thing was ridiculous. We were sent to Oriente Province and we encountered heavy resistance at times with a number of dead and wounded. We took a number of rebel prisoners, but we freed them soon. The whole thing was ridiculous.

---

[170] Rosendo Collazo, Cuban Army Colonel whose victory at La Lucha marked the beginning of the end for the "Chambelona" rebels.

[171] Ibrahím Consuegra. Cuban Army Colonel who together with Colonel Collazo, defeated Gómez's supporters at La Lucha.

[172] The Battle of Caicaje took place on March 18, 1917, culminating in Gómez's defeat and capture.

ANA AURORA RECIO: I remember the "Chambelona" revolt quite well because my father was arrested in Camagüey. What happened there was that the Liberals arrested Conservative Governor Bernabé Sánchez[173]. The Conservatives, trying to persuade the Liberals to release Bernabé, arrested my father, one of my father's friend, Manuel Cavada, and a priest.

My father told us that he had fun while under arrest, because Don Manuel was really scared. My father said that Don Manuel used to hide behind rocking chairs, sofas, anything he could find. My father, then, would tell him: "Hey, quit hiding! If a bullet hits you, it simply hits you and that's it. There's no point in hiding, so just come around and sit like the rest of us. Besides, we have no problems here because there is a priest with us."

RICARDO COBIÁN: During the "Chambelona", I founded a newspaper, "La Izquierda Liberal," ("The Liberal Left"). It was a militant newspaper seeking reforms and criticizing political corruption. Since Menocal had committed electoral fraud, I wrote an article entitled "¡Basta ya, General!" ("Enough is Enough, General!"). Nothing happened to me and I continued with my militancy.

---

[173] Bernabé Sánchez Batista. Conservative Governor of Camagüey during the "Chambelona" uprising.

THE 1921 ECONOMIC CRISIS

CELESTINO SUÁREZ: I experienced the 1921 economic crisis[174]. I was working at the Banco Español. The members of the Board of Directors had stocks worth only a few cents, but they inflated their value and cashed in the money. It wasn't happening just at that bank; it was happening all over Cuba. There was rampant speculation and things got out of control. Menocal had promised to put an end to all of that, but he didn't do a damned thing. The Americans knew about it, but they didn't do a thing either. Suddenly, one day, the whole thing came tumbling down and bankruptcy became the order of the day.

In Cienfuegos, there lived a Spanish guy named José María Fontela. He was a good man, but he was the epitome of bruteness. One day, he went to the bank to withdraw 400 *pesos* he had in his bank account. However, bank officials told him to come later. Fontela threw a tantrum and began yelling: "Give me my 400 *pesos*! I put them here and they got to come out of here!" The officials were trying to calm him down and they were telling him: "Fontela, come later, please come later." Fontela replied: "Why don't you ask your mother to come later. Give me my *pesos*!" Things got so out of hand that the officials gave him the money just to get out of the way.

Unfortunately, there were lots of Spaniards like my father who lost more than 20,000 *pesos* and there were many Spanish food store owners who had no money to pay import customs, so their merchandise all got spoiled at the custom houses. It was just obscene because those people were Spanish immigrants who had

---

[174] Financial crisis brought about by a drop in sugar prices in the world market and excessive speculation. Eleven of the major banks in Cuba went bankrupt as a result of the crisis.

worked very hard and practically in one day, they lost everything they had.

Celestino Suárez with wife Josefa, 1985
(Courtesy of Clarisa Miller)

MACHADO'S DICTATORSHIP AND THE HOTEL NACIONAL EPISODE

CARLOS MONTERO: Machado was a great president during his first four years. He was a popular and very positive individual. He was very well organized and since he wanted to industrialize Cuba in order to limit American dependency, he imposed duties on American products.[175] The Americans, as expected, didn't like that, and were upset with Machado. Later on, they would get even with him.

Machado was a womanizer, but he did a splendid job as president during his first four years. The problem with Machado were his cronies who ruined everything he did. They flattered him and flattery brought his downfall. Human beings like to be flattered but there's got to be a limit to it. In Machado's case, flattery clogged up his brain and he became an egomaniac. Even the University of Havana faculty started to kiss his ass, and he loved every minute of it.

Regarding his relationship with the Army, he thought he was its master. He promoted officers who kissed his ass and demoted or relieved of their command those who didn't. Many of us who were junior officers didn't like to kiss his ass, so we just weren't promoted. Some of the older officers began to get fed up with Machado's ego and there were talks of coups and uprisings. However, the younger officers like me, even if we didn't like him, didn't want any of that stuff because Lezama had taught us never to get involved in politics.

As time went on, things began to get bad for Machado. He thought he could always count on the Army and began to commit

---

[175] During Machado's administration, Cuba went from 4th to 16th place as an importer of American products.

atrocities against the general population. He began to have a lot of problems with university students because they are always outspoken. They began to organize protest marches against his abuses and the police started to beat them up. Some of them even got killed and people began to turn against him.

There was another group that contributed to Machado's downfall and those were the Americans. Machado was doing things that the Americans didn't want him to do, so they sent Sumner Welles[176] as Ambassador to Cuba. He was sort of like a show off but he was Roosevelt's man who was sent to put pressure on Machado. So, with the student pressure on one side, and the American pressure on the other side, Machado began to feel the heat. Then the Army turned on him. Machado had no other alternative than to leave the country. By the way, he is buried here in Miami.

MANUEL GARCÍA IGLESIAS: Machado's downfall was a slow process in which the Americans played their part. Machado, despite his faults, wanted to end Cuban economic dependency on the United States and he was doing so. The Americans retaliated by imposing a two cent per pound duty on Cuban sugar. That law was the Hawley-Smoot Tariff.[177] Since the Cuban economy was largely dependent on sugar and the United States was its principal customer, the tariff hit the Cuban economy very hard. A short while later, Cuban sugar prices dropped a cent per pound in the world market.

---

[176] Benjamin Sumner Welles (1892-1961). American Ambassador to Cuba (1933-1934) who played a key role in Machado's downfall. A close friend of President Franklin D. Roosevelt, he was American Embassy Secretary in Buenos Aires, Argentina, prior to his appointment in Havana. Born in New York City on October 14, 1892, he died in Bernardsville, New Jersey on September 24, 1961.

[177] The Hawley-Smoot Tariff was approved by Congress in 1930. It imposed a two-cent duty per pound on imported Cuban sugar. The tariff coincided with the 1.04 cent drop per pound of sugar in the world market.

As a result, the Cuban economy was in a precarious situation and Machado made things worse by issuing a decree[178] calling for elections. They were rigged, extending his presidency until 1935. People just couldn't tolerate that anymore and reacted violently through bombing campaigns, assassination attempts and other forms of terrorism. Additionally, protest marches were a dime a dozen. Even though most of them were peaceful, the police reacted with brute force.

All of these activities would pave the way for an army coup with American blessings. Sumner Welles began contacting key sectors of Cuban society, warning them of a possible American intervention. Finally, he succeeded in convincing the armed forces under Alberto Herrera[179] that it was necessary to stage a coup. However, before the coup, there was a general strike. The Communists tried to break the strike by asking Machado to legalize the Communist Party in exchange for breaking the strike. Machado didn't accept the offer, but it was too late. Things got out of hand for him and he left the country.

I contributed to Machado's downfall because I was always against him. Because of my opposition to Machado, I had fled Cuba for Miami on a boat using a false passport. Colonel Bazán[180]

---

[178] The decree known as the "Prórroga de Poderes" ("Presidential Powers Extension"), was passed by the Machado-controlled Cuban Congress in 1927 in violation of article 115 of the 1901 Cuban Constitution. The law extended Machado's presidential powers and term in office. It was responsible for igniting the revolt against Machado.

[179] Alberto Herrera y Franchi (1874-1954). General and Secretary of War and Navy. Herrera followed Welles's plan of deposing Machado and on August 12, 1933; Machado resigned as president. Machado fled to the Bahamas with his closest collaborators and later established himself in Miami, Florida. Herrera, not trusted by different elements of Cuban society, was Acting President for only one day, and went into exile, but returned years later to Cuba. Born in San Antonios de las Vueltas, Las Villas Province, on September 1, 1874, he died in Havana, on September 19, 1954.

[180] Celestino Bazán Novo. Colonel in the Cuban Liberation Army and Interim Governor of Havana Province.

who was in the United States, ordered me to go to Cuba on a mission. Unfortunately, immediately after the seaplane docked in Havana, police officers were waiting for me because someone had blown the whistle. They arrested me and took me to Ainciart[181] who was the Police Chief.

I don't know how I was able to save my life because Ainciart was a psycho and an assassin. His hands were always trembling with rage and all he did was to kill people. I remember that the next day I was at the Príncipe[182] when a bomb exploded in the morning right across from Doctor Ferrara's[183] home. Ainciart and his men avenged the incident by assassinating 32 men, presumed of being revolutionaries.

I was in jail for 78 days, but I was freed through Sumner Welles's mediation. After my release, I stayed in Havana until the August 12, 1933 coup. Since I was connected to the "Directorio Estudantil Revolucionario" [184] ("The Student Revolutionary Directorate"), I became very busy that day. I was carrying a Mauser rifle and ammunition belts because the "Directorio" had ordered me and 12 others to take over one of Machado's residencies near the University of Havana. When we reached the residence, we peppered the place with bullets because it was thought to be full of his followers. When we finished shooting all over the place, two very old police officers who could hardly walk came out with their hands up, and we simply just let them go.

In 1931, he staged an ill-fated uprising against Machado in Oriente Province. After its failure, he escaped to Miami, Florida.

[181] Antonio B. Ainciart, Machado's Chief of Police, noted for his cruelty and numerous atrocities.

[182] Castle-fortress in Havana built during Spanish colonial times which was later used by different Cuban governments as a prison.

[183] Orestes Ferrara (1876-1972). Colonel in the Cuban Liberation Army who became a Congressman, Ambassador to the United States, and Cuban Secretary of State during Machado's dictatorship. Born in Naples, Italy, on July 18, 1876, he died in Rome, Italy, on February 16, 1972..

[184] Anti-Machado organization composed of University of Havana students.

That day, I witnessed several of Machado's supporters' residencies being sacked. I remember the people setting "La Gerona" Bakery on fire because it was said that its owner, Secundino López, was a Machado supporter. I also witnessed the sacking of Averhoff's[185] residence. The people were throwing the furniture out of the windows and setting them on fire.

The incident that shocked me the most was seeing how the mob dragged Ainciart's corpse through the streets of Havana. He had escaped dressed as a woman and was hiding in someone's home, right in the kitchen. Apparently, someone identified him and a mob just dragged him out.[186] It was horrible what they did to him, but on the other hand, people just wanted to get even with him for all the atrocities he had committed.

MARIO VEGA: I was only a kid when Machado was president and only 14 when he was overthrown. In analyzing Machado's presidency, he, during his first four years in office, was one of the best presidents in Cuban history. He was a nationalist who tried to industrialize Cuba and for that reason, we must tip our hats to him. However, in Cuba, when there was a president who was a nationalist, "foreign interests" would begin to turn the screws and make things difficult for him.

I really think that there will never be a totally independent Cuba because there is a lack of citizenship among Cubans. Countries are measured by their citizens' qualities and in Cuba there were many *guerrilleros*[187] who didn't know the meaning of the word Fatherland. They didn't know what dignity meant or what

---

[185] Octavio Averhoff was a former Rector of the University of Havana who was Secretary of the Treasury during Machado's dictatorship. After Machado's downfall, he fled to exile in the United States.

[186] According to sources, Ainciart committed suicide and his corpse was dragged through the streets of Havana and mutilated.

[187] Derogatory term given to Cubans who fought for the Spanish during the Cuban War of Independence.

sacrifices meant. All they were interested in was demagoguery and in being powerful and rich.

Now, going back to Machado, after those four years, he turned into a dictator. People had to do something because they were going hungry and had no freedom. No government in the world has the right to keep people on their knees.

Although I was very young, I recall the struggle against Machado. My brother, for example, was an ABC[188] member and I even knew Martínez Sáenz[189] Saladrigas,[190] and other leaders because they once met at my home. Over in the garden, my family used to hide ABC propaganda. One evening, we even saw the "Hora Fantasma" ("Phantom Hour") car. It was a car which transmitted anti-Machado propaganda. Despite Machado's police's efforts, they were never able to catch the guy because the car moved undetected throughout Havana. I remember the day Machado was brought down. Everyone went out on the streets to celebrate. I saw Anciart's body being dragged through the streets of Havana. A bit later they hung it from a lamppost at the University of Havana. I witnessed people sacking "Pepito" Izquierdo's[191] home which was near the Telephone Company in Marianao, a Havana suburb,

---

[188] Anti-Machado secret organization founded by Joaquín Martínez Sáenz and Carlos Saladrigas. Composed of middle-class professionals, its goals were to bring democracy, social justice, and economic independence to Cuba

[189] Joaquín Martínez Sáenz (1900-1970). Lawyer and one of the founders of the ABC. Martínez Sáenz became President of Cuba's National Bank in the 1950s during Batista's dictatorship. After the triumph of the Cuban Revolution, he was condemned to 15 years in prison. Following his release, he went into exile in the United States. He was born in Güira de Melena, Havana Province- in 1900, and died in Miami, Florida, in 1970.

[190] Carlos Saladrigas y Zayas (1900-1956). Lawyer and one of the founders of the ABC. After Machado's downfall, he became a noted Cuban politician occupying several key posts such as Senator (1936-1940), and Prime Minister (1940-1942). In 1944, he was an unsuccessful candidate for the Cuban presidency. Born in Havana, on October 13, 1900, he died in said city, on April 15, 1956.

[191] Jose "Pepito" Izquierdo was named Mayor of Havana in 1931. He fled to the Bahamas with Machado, on August 12, 1933.

which was actually, a big city. There was nothing left in that place; people even took out the floor tiles. Those "porristas"[192] who had managed to hide (but were caught) were dragged out of the hiding places, beaten, and later killed.

The irony of the struggle against Machado is that it was all in vain because of Fulgencio Batista's betrayal. He staged a coup on September 4, not even a month after Machado's downfall, destroyed all of Cuba's institutions, and legalized the *Partido Socialista Popular*, as the Communist Party was officially known. It's because of Batista that we now have Fidel Castro[193]. Batista was such a coward that once he had stolen millions of dollars and things heated up for him. He told his followers: "Every man for himself," and left the country. He really set the table up for another betrayal and that's Castro's betrayal.

I believe that Castro got in power because people were tired of so much demagoguery and Batista's corruption. A number of Cubans only thought of enriching themselves and being "kissy, kissy" with the Americans. However, nothing is comparable to Castro's betrayal. He handed Cuba to the Russians who are the biggest sons-of-bitches in the world.

ENRIQUE CASERO: I was in Havana during Machado's downfall, but I can assure you that the situation in Santiago was no different. Later, I saw people dragging Victor Vizcay out in the street. He was the mayor of an Oriente town called San Luis during Machado's dictatorship. They said people lynched him in retaliation for squealing on seven anti-Machado conspirators who were later

---

[192] Name given by the Cuban people to the "Liga Patriótica" ("Patriotic League"), a pro-Machado vigilante organization composed mostly of common criminals and thugs. The word *porra* in Spanish means club or nightstick.

[193] Fidel Castro Ruz (1926-2016). Leader of the Cuban Revolution who overthrew dictator Fulgencio Batista, on January 1, 1959. Hated and despised by Cuban exiles, he ruled Cuba with an iron fist until his death. Born in Oriente Province, on August 13, 1926, he died in Havana on November 25, 2016. A Communist dictatorship continues to rule Cuba, under Raúl Castro Ruz, Fidel Castro's younger brother.

executed. Vizcay was jailed for a few days after Machado's downfall, but the minute he was freed, a mob dragged him down Marina Street all the way to Santiago's cemetery. When they reached the cemetery, he was still alive and they proceeded to lynch him. He was black. I met him once and he seemed to be a nice guy, but apparently, he had enemies.

CARLOS MONTERO: When Machado fell, he said: "After me, all hell is going to break loose." He was right because Batista staged a coup on September 4. A group of officers, including myself, didn't like Batista and as a result, the Hotel Nacional Episode took place. We were very close to Sanguily,[194] the Chief of Staff who was convalescing from surgery. A mob of noncommissioned officers led by Belisario Hernández,[195] attacked his home. After the incident, Sanguily had internal bleeding, thus complicating his recovery. A group of officers decided to transfer him to the Hotel Nacional because his son was the hotel's doctor and he was going to be well attended there.

After transferring him to the hotel, his son managed to get him moved to one of the towers. Espino, one of his aides, and I would go to see him every day to take care of him. Since Sanguily was not in good health, other officers used to visit him daily. Batista was afraid of us because we were professional soldiers, so, he ordered his men to block access to the hotel for us. We were there, but a few of our officers secretly got through the blockade, carrying rifles and ammunition. All in all, there were about 20 of us there.

---

[194] Julio Sanguily (1879-1935). Chief of the Cuban Air Corps, he assumed the post of Chief of Staff of the Cuban Armed Forces after Machado's downfall, and following the resignation of General Alberto Herrera. Batista removed him from his post after his coup on September 4, 1933.

[195] Belisario Hernández was a Cuban Army sergeant who was later named Chief of Police by Batista.

Since Batista wanted to destroy the Officer Corps, he ordered the attack on the hotel.[196] The fighting took place around five in the morning. It lasted until three in the afternoon when we surrendered because we ran out of ammunition. We only suffered one dead. His name was Alberti.[197] He was one of the officers and died from shrapnel wounds. Batista's men had lots of casualties because there were many among us who had been members of the Cuban Olympic Rifle Team and they were excellent marksmen.

Batista's soldiers got mad after our surrender when they realized that we just had only one single casualty. Just when we were walking towards the trucks, they began shooting us in our backs and sides. They killed and wounded some of our comrades.[198] The wounded were taken to the Calixto García Hospital[199] and the non-wounded were taken to La Cabaña Fortress. My uncle was shot in his side and the bullet came out of his back. That's how Colonel Céspedes[200] and Severito Piña[201] got killed. All of that episode happened in just one day, October 2, 1933.

After being imprisoned for awhile, Batista tried to fix things up and we were invited to rejoin the Army, but hardly any of us accepted the invitation. We were professional soldiers. We were officers and Batista was nothing more than low-rent trash.

---

[196] Controversy still surrounds the Hotel Nacional Episode which took place on October 2, 1933. The most authoritative version maintains that officers set quarters at the Hotel Nacional, Havana's prime hotel, to ask Ambassador Welles, a hotel resident to intervene in reinstating deposed President Carlos Manuel de Céspedes and General Sanguily. There is another version which maintains that officers gathered at the hotel to stage a coup against Batista in cooperation with the ABC.

[197] According to sources, Alberti was not the officer killed. The officer killed was Lieutenant Abelardo Fernández.

[198] After their surrender, Hernandez's soldiers killed 10 officers in cold blood.

[199] Havana's largest hospital.

[200] Lieutenant Colonel Miguel A. Céspedes.

[201] Army Captain Evelio Piña.

THIRD PART

UNDER A FOREIGN SUN

MY LIFE IN THE UNITED STATES

LORENZO ZEQUEIRA: I'm fine here and I am thankful to the country, but that sense of love that we had in Cuba doesn't exist here. For example, when I use to leave home for work, all of the neighbors would come out to wish me well, saying: "Lorencito!" "Lorencito!" Here, I live in an eight-apartment complex and no one comes out to greet me, wish me well or anything. In fact, I only know one neighbor.

There is neither the love nor the affinity in this country that we had in Cuba and that's the thing I miss the most about Cuba. Now, I think this is due to this country's way of life, because those of us who are now living here have also lost that sense of brotherhood that we had in Cuba.

RODOLFO SOTOLONGO: I'll be grateful to this country until the day I die. I only have nothing but thankfulness and praise for the way it has welcomed us and for granting those of us who are doctors the opportunity to renew our licenses, practice medicine, and live honorably.

FELIPE ROLOFF: I can't complain about this country. I came here as an exile. I live here, and I've had the opportunity to educate my daughters here. I've worked very hard I'm not rich, but I own property. I have no complaints about this country, but I don't feel well here. I feel that I'm in someone else's home because this country is not my home. When one isn't in one's home, one doesn't feel well.

JOSEFINA PÉREZ: I live well here because I have all of my children, grandchildren and great-grandchildren here in Miami. As a matter of fact, one of my granddaughters is a Representative in the Florida House of Representatives.[202] I'm so happy about her because she is very smart.

The only thing I can't understand about this country is its food. Here people go out and get a "hamburgue" (hamburger) and that "hamburgue" fills them up for the whole day. In Cuba, we didn't do that; we ate well. One would eat soup, all kinds of beef, rice and beans. Cuban food was very nutritious. However, over here kids are fed "hamburgues" from the day they are born. Long ago, people lived longer and were healthier because they ate better. Here, everything is solved with a "hamburgue."

ENRIQUE CASERO: I live here like a coffee plantation millionaire. I'm poor, but the most important thing in life is to have friends and the few remaining friends I have - my friends are dying - are here in this country.

MARIO VEGA: I am honored to live in the greatest country in the world, the United States of America. This country is the most powerful country in the world. I'm thankful to the American people for their sense of human kindness and having welcomed so many immigrants from different nations. I'm an American citizen and I'll gladly offer my life for this country.

RICARDO COBIÁN: I live very well here. The government has given me a place to live. Actually, it's owned by the Dominican Friars, but the government subsidizes it. The elderly are treated very well here, but for us elderly citizens, there is no return to Cuba. We are simply too old.

---

[202] Ileana Ros Lehtinen, the first Hispanic woman ever to be elected to the Florida House of Representatives (1982), the Florida Senate (1986), and the US House of Representatives (1989). She was born in Havana, on July 15, 1952. Representing Florida's 27th Congressional District, she is Florida's most senior representative to the US House of Representatives. From 2011 through 2013, she chaired the House Foreign Affairs Committee. She is known for her opposition to the Castro regime and championing human rights.

REFLECTIONS

JOSEFINA PÉREZ: I give thanks to God every day for giving me health, peace and calmness. I'm close to my family - we get along very well - and that's a great feeling. Everyone should be thankful to God for helping us, and for accompanying us. Generally, I say the rosary 4 to 6 times a day. At times, I say to myself: "God is going to get mad at me for invoking his help so much." However, all I ask is for health, peace and calm, and for keeping my family united.

Josefina Pérez, c. 1957
(Courtesy of Eddie Fiol)

RODOLFO SOTOLONGO: At my age, I have to be thankful for waking up in the morning. The past is gone, and the future for those of us who are old is to wake up alive when morning comes.

CARLOS MONTERO: At my age, life is like a falling leaf and the only thing left are our reminiscences. I love to remember the past. The only problem is that remembering the great past moments, go out quickly; they simply fly out of your mind.

I'm now experiencing things that are common to older people. Now, my family bosses me around telling me: "Don't eat this !" "Don't go out alone!" " Do this or that!" I'm a strong-willed person who doesn't like to be bossed around. There is nothing that pisses me off more than being bossed around. Who the hell was going to tell me when I lived in Cuba: "Don't do this or that!" "Man, that isn't living at all!" But, well, one has to continue on.

HORTENSIA LÓPEZ: I'm already 95 years old. I have lived a sane life; I've never smoked, and I've never drank, and no one in my family has ever been a drunk. If anyone wants to reach my age, I advise them never to smoke and live a peaceful life. At my age, my doctor's only restriction for me is not to be around when they are smoking because secondhand smoke is a killer.

CEFERINO GARCÍA: My life has been one of sacrifices and I don't mind having lived a life full of sacrifices. I remember people coming over to me and telling me: "Hey, you got to enjoy life a little bit more." I would always answer: "Yes, but now is the time to sacrifice." Life has proven that I was right, because now, I live well. Now, that I'm old, I don't have to sacrifice.

VÍCTOR VEGA CEBALLOS: If I were to live my life again, I would do the same things over and over. I have no regrets over the things that I have done. My only regret is about the things that I haven't done.

I have served my country by the way I was educated, and the way my family was educated. I have served those in need, because the rich haven't needed my services. They take care of themselves and eat well, so no one has to feed them. Therefore, they don't need my services. As a man who was in public office[203] I have helped many people. There were those who were my supporters and were on my side and one day, they left me. Although I appointed some of them to their posts, they no longer supported me. I appointed them because they needed the jobs, not because they had supported me.

Life is like a rock quarry where there are lots of stones, so people can come out to pick those stones to throw at others. Fortunately, I've been a well-respected individual but once, someone, indirectly, threw a stone at me by saying that he never switched political parties in his life. I know why that was being said, because I had switched political parties. I simply replied: "In life there are two types of people: those who have no ideas, and those who are fine with their ideas. But there are those who want change, and if they want change, they have to change their ideas." It's simply human nature to change, and I did that.

I'm pleased with my life. I traveled many roads and like a traveler, I see things like one who has visited a place, never ever to return to that place. I write because writing is an escape mechanism for being out of my country and fully knowing that there is no return. So, it's like being strangled. However, one must realize that life never stops. At times, there is a bit of a traffic jam, but it continues on. Human beings will always go forward, always forward.

---

[203] Víctor Vega Ceballos served as a Representative from Camagüey to the Cuban House of Representatives during the administration of President Carlos Prío Socarras (1948-1952). During Batista's presidency (1940-1944), he served as Attorney General (1940-1941) and Secretary of Interior (1941-1942).

REFERENCES

Álvarez, Díaz, José, et al. *Cuba: Geopolítica y pensamiento económico.* Miami: Colegio de Economistas de Cuba en el Exilio, 1964.

Arrowsmith, William and Roger Shattuck, eds. *The Craft and Context of Translation.* Austin: Universiy of Texas Press, 1961.

Baker, Mona. *The other Words: A Coursebook in Translation.* London: Routledge, 1992.

Beals, Carleton. *The Crime of Cuba.* Philadelphia: J. B. Lippincott and Company, 1933.

Betancourt, Enrique C. *Apuntes para la Historia: Radio, Televisión y Farándula de la Cuba de Ayer.* San Juan, Ramallo, 1986.

Bueno, Salvador. *Cuban Legends.* Princeton: Markus Wiener Publishers, 2007.

Catholic Encyclopedia. New York: Robert Appleton Company, 1912.

Chapman, Charles. *A History of the Cuban Republic.* New York: The Macmillan Company, 1927.

Chidsey, Donald. *The Spanish-American War.* New York: Crown Publishers, 1971.

Collazo, Enrique. *La Revolución de agosto de 1906.* La Habana: Imprenta C. Martínez y Cía., 1907.

Cuyás, Arturo. *Appleton's New Cuyás Dictionary.* Englewood Cliffs: Prentice-Hall, 1992.

Díaz Alaya, Cristóbal. *Música cubana: Del Areyto a la Nueva Trova.* San Juan: Editorial Cubanacán, 1981.

Diccionario de la Lengua Española. Madrid: Real Academia Española. 1970.

Encinosa, Enrique. *Azúcar y Chocolate: historia del boxeo cubano.* Miami: Ediciones Universal, 2004.

Fermoselle, Rafael. *Política y color en Cuba: La Guerrita de 1912*. Montevideo: Ediciones Géminis, 1974.

Fernández, José B. *Los Abuelos: Historia oral cubana*. Miami: Ediciones Universal, 1987.

Fernández Soneira, Teresita. *Cuba: historia de la educación católica, 1582-1961*. Miami: Ediciones Universal, 1977.

Gómez, Máximo. *Diario de Campaña*. Santo Domingo: Alfa y Omega, 1975.

Guerra y Sánchez, Ramiro. *Historia de la nación cubana*. La Habana: Editorial de la nación cubana, 1952.

Hyatt, Verrill. *Cuba, Past and Present*. New York: Dodd, Mead and Company, 1920.

Lazcano, Andrés. *Las Constituciones de Cuba*. Madrid: Ediciones Cultura Hispánica, 1952.

Le Riverend, Julio. *La República*. La Habana: Editorial de Ciencias Sociales, 1975.

Lluría de O'Higgins, María Josefa. *A Taste of Old Cuba*. New York: William Morrow Cookbooks, 1994.

Mackay, Nancy. *Curating Oral Histories: From Interview to Archive*. Walnut Creek: Left Coast Press, 2007.

Martínez Ortiz, Rafael. *Cuba: Los primeros años de independencia*. Paris: Editorial Le Livre Libre, 1929.

Masó, Calixto. *Historia de Cuba*. Miami: Ediciones Universal, 1976.

Miró Argenter, José. *Crónicas de la Guerra*. La Habana, 1909.

Morales, Vidal. *Iniciadores y primeros mátires de la revolución*. La Habana: Consejo Nancional de Cultura, 1963.

Okler, Daniel. *The Ultimate Baseball Book*. Boston: Houghton-Mifflin, 1984.

Paz, Ramón. *Índice de relaciones de méritos y servicios conservados en la sección de Consejos*. Madrid: Archivo Histórico Nacional, 1943.

Pérez, Louis A. "Vagrants, Beggars and Bandits: Social Origins of Cuban Separation, 1878-1895." *The American Historical Review.* Vol. 90, No. 5 (December, 1985): 1092-1121.

Phillips, Ruby Hart. *Cuba: Island of Paradox.* New York: McDowell Obolensky, 1959.

Pichardo Moya, Esteban. *Diccionario provincial casi razonado de vozes y frases cubanas.* La Habana: Editoriales de Ciencias Sociales, 1975.

Riera Hernández, Mario. *Cuba Republicana 1899-1958.* Miami: Editorial A I P, 1974.

Ritchie, Donald A. *Doing Oral History.* New York: Oxford University Press, 2003.

Sánchez-Boudy, José. *Diccionario de Cubanismos más usuales.* Miami: Ediciones Universal, 1978.

Santeiro, Francisco. *Gerardo Machado y Morales: Ocho años de lucha.* Miami: Ediciones Históricas Cubanas, 1982.

Santovenia, Emeterio y Raúl M. Shelton. *Cuba y su historia.* Miami: Rome Press, 1967.

Terwilleger, L. Roy. *Cuban Folk-Lore.* London: Forgotten Books, 2015.

Thomas, Hugh. *Cuba: The Pursuit of Freedom.* New York: Harper and Row, 1971.

_____ *Cuba: A History.* London: Penguin Books, 2010.

Varela Zequeira, Eduardo. *La Politica en 1905 o episodios de una lucha electoral.* La Habana: Rambla y Bouza, 1905.

Weems, John. *The Fate of the Maine.* New York: Henry Holt and Company, 1958.

Webster's New Twentieth Century Dictionary of the English Language. New York: Collins World, 1977.

Wright, Irene. *Cuba.* New York: MacMillan, 1910.

www.ingramcontent.com/pod-product-compliance
Lightning Source LLC
Chambersburg PA
CBHW030518080526
44586CB00011B/246